D1793759

Grand River Country Trails 2

by Katherine Jacob

National Library of Canada Cataloguing in Publication Data

Jacob, Katherine, 1967-
  Grand River country trails "2": / by Katherine Jacob

Includes index.
Copyright © 2004 Katherine Jacob
ISBN 0-9683389-4-1

1. Trails - Ontario - Grand River Region - Guidebooks. 2. Trails - Ontario - Waterloo (Regional municipality) - Guidebooks. 3. Trails - Ontario - Wellington (County) - Guidebooks. 4. Grand River Region (Ont.) - Guidebooks. 5. Waterloo (Ont.: Regional municipality) - Guidebooks. 6. Wellington (Ont.: County) - Guidebooks. I. Grand River Conservation Foundation II. Title.

FC3095.G72A3 2004   917.13'42045   C2004-901911-2

Printed by Ampersand Printing, Guelph, Ontario

This book is for information purposes only, and the author and publisher take no responsibility for, nor guarantee, the accuracy of all the information contained in the book. Trail conditions may change, vary and be re-routed over time. Man-made obstacles, obstructions, alterations or new construction on or near the trails may also change or affect conditions as described in this book. The author and publisher cannot be held responsible for any thefts, problems, injuries or misfortunes that occur from use of the material in this book. Remember that safety is a personal responsibility. Note: maps are not to scale.

This is a companion book to the Grand River Country Trails book , first published in 1999 by The Record.

Author: Katherine Jacob
Page Layout and Map Design: Lara Vujanic
Cover photo: Rockwood Conservation Area
Photographed by: John Opiola

Published by: Grand River Conservation Foundation
                                 Box 729
                                 400 Clyde Rd.
                                 Cambridge ON   N1R5W6
                                 (519) 621-2761
                                 www.grandriver.ca

Maps produced by the Grand River Conservation Authority with contributions from:
                                 The Record
                                 The City of Brantford
                                 The City of Cambridge
                                 The City of Guelph
                                 The City of Kitchener
                                 The City of Waterloo
                                 Ruthven Park National Historic Site

All proceeds of book sales will be shared by the Grand River Conservation Foundation and The Record newspaper, to respectively support local trail development and improvement projects of the GRCA, and The Record's Playground Renewal Fund.

Grand River Country Trails 2

THE RECORD

by Katherine Jacob

Other books by Katherine Jacob

Grand River Country Trails

44 Country Trails

Bruce Peninsula Trails

The Best of the Bruce Trail

Oak Ridges Moraine Trails

See www.katherinejacob.ca

PHOTOGRAPH AND ILLUSTRATION CREDIT

Elizabeth Bourque - page 92
The City of Brantford - Tourism Brantford - page 40
Cambridge Tourism - page 61
Ken Fields - pages 8, 14, 15, 21, 31, 66
Grand River Conservation Authority - pages 18, 26, 34, 36, 42, 48, 54, 56, 58, 60, 70, 71, 74, 75, 78, 80, 82, 95
Tourism Haldimand - page 68
Katherine Jacob - pages 32, 35, 46, 47, 51, 52, 55, 62, 72, 73, 76, 77, 88
Mathew McCarthy - pages 20, 38, 44, 50, 86, 90
Carolyn McLeod - page 22
Bob McMullen - pages 33, 43, 57
Andrew Mills - pages 17, 27, 39, 59
John Opiola - cover and page 64
Lisa Totzke - pages 16, 30, 84, 94
Robert Wilson - pages 24, 28

This book is dedicated to my younger, but "older" brother, for bringing home my first kitten and most importantly, for teaching me how to ride a bike.

A special thanks, always, to all readers who have supported The Record's Trail Markers column throughout the years and to all my friends and family who walked these trails with me and provided support, valuable information and suggestions, especially Mom, John, Moragh, Devin, Aaron and Leanne.

Thank you to the Grand River Conservation Authority for their support of my work during the last decade, especially the editorial and design team on this book: Ralph Beaumont for sharing the vision and pulling all the loose ends together; Lara Vujanic for imaginative design and patience with the many text and visual elements involved with this book; Dave Schultz for his thorough editing and attention to detail; all Grand River Conservation Authority staff; trail association volunteers and K-W Field Naturalists; especially Chris Earley, Dan Schneider, Duane Brown, Peter Wetherup, Len Fay, Bob McMullen, for time and energy.

Thank you to The Record, for supporting my column during the last decade, Aubrey Walters for her continued support, and especially my editor, Carol Jankowski, for believing in Trail Markers, for her professional expertise, commitment and thoughtfulness throughout the years.

Since this is a book from the region where I grew up, I'd like to thank my parents for raising me in a wonderful community; my brothers, sister and friends for exploring the countryside with me; and three special school teachers who strongly encouraged my love for writing: Nancy Rotozinski, Joy Eichholz and Edith Janke.

TABLE OF CONTENTS

Trail Descriptions

Trail Tips

INTRODUCTION

As Trail Markers edges close to a decade of running as a column featuring nature trails in the Grand River Country region, I'm amazed at the number of trails there are, and how many are continuously being built. It's a credit to the vision of the Grand River Conservation Authority (GRCA), municipalities, local land management agencies, and tireless community groups and volunteers.

This year the Grand celebrates its tenth year as a Canadian Heritage River, and in its honour we're releasing this book featuring another 40 of the best trails in our region. All of these trails are located in the Grand River Watershed, an area influenced by the Grand, which flows south from the Dundalk Highlands for 298 kilometres to its mouth at Lake Erie. Each trail is chosen for its natural value, seasonal features and proximity to regional cities and towns.

The work I've done for trails and natural spaces in this community has always been with the hope that nature will be valued and therefore preserved. Through the sales of the first Grand River Country Trails book, more than $30,000 was raised to build a section of the Walter Bean Grand River Trail. It is my hope that sales of Grand River Country Trails "2" will exceed this amount, to be used by The Record for its local Playground Renewal Fund, and by the Grand River Conservation Foundation for their ongoing trail building and improvement program in cooperation with the GRCA.

Throughout the years that I've been writing the column, readers have shared their love for hiking and nature with me. Some have said the columns become regular family outings, others are interested in quiet moments where they draw inspiration.

There is a bonding that takes place in nature, either with yourself or others. It is the quiet and simplicity, I think. On trails you walk away from problems, responsibilities and obligations into a place where bird calls, wind song, tumbling leaves, and blossoming flowers soothe your spirit. Such uninterrupted time is the ultimate luxury.

Enjoy the Trails!

Katherine

p.s. Whatever your own personal connections with nature and trails are, please share them with me at www.katherinejacob.ca

Letter from the Editor

Why go for a walk? The answer is simple: because it's such a wonderfully versatile pastime. You can walk alone or with a group, in almost any weather, in almost any location, and the price couldn't be better. The workout builds up your bones and, if you're waist-watching, it helps tone muscles and helps your heart. It opens up vistas along creeks and lakes, through forests and valleys, even in the heart of a city, that you'd miss speeding past in a car.

And while it exercises your body, a walk or hike feeds your soul. It offers time to think and to dream - or to escape from your thoughts. There's time and space to talk, or to be silent.

The better question, then, is why not walk?

In the years since 1996 when Katherine Jacob began writing her popular weekly Trail Markers column for The Record in Kitchener, walking and hiking have become trendy. In Grand River country, the 75-kilometre (47 mile) Walter Bean Grand River Trail has been all but completed. It's a tribute to what philanthropy, volunteerism and supporters large and small, corporate and individual, accomplished for communities strung along one of Canada's scenic heritage rivers.

Land planners now incorporate networks of walking paths in new residential areas, knowing their environmental and marketing appeal will resonate with young fitness-conscious families.

With one of Katherine's trail guides in hand, you'll appreciate the bird songs heard all around as you walk. You'll feel the soft pine needles underfoot, warm to the sunlight glinting through a canopy of branches overhead, pause to admire the wildflowers tucked among the rocks. The experience will leave you more determined than ever to protect this land.

So turn off that cellphone, choose a route and get walking. Discover the world as Katherine Jacob sees it. And find out why she has made trail guides as popular as a good novel.

Carol Jankowski

Carol Jankowski
Life Editor
The Record

How To Use This Guide

This guide offers brief descriptions and detailed maps for each trail. A loop trail means a return to the starting point via another route. A linear trail returns to the starting point via the same route.

Some trails have parking lots at start and end points plus other access locations, allowing hikers to arrange a car shuttle so they don't have to return to their starting point - an important feature if the trail is long.

If there is a link with a long-distance trail such as the Grand Valley or Trans Canada Trail, it will be mentioned in the trail description and noted in the Trail Features section at the back of the book. For information on a long-distance trail, consult their guides (addresses and phone numbers are provided).

Trails are marked in various ways. The Grand Valley Trail system follows white blazes of paint on trees, rocks and poles. A single blaze means the trail continues in the same direction. Two blazes, one above the other, indicate a change of direction. If the top blaze is offset, this indicates the direction of the turn. A blue blaze indicates a side trail.

Symbols for trail features and facilities appear on individual trail maps. The "Trail Features" matrix in the back of this book lists permitted uses. Only a few trails offer track-set skiing, but snowshoes can be used in winter on most walking trails.

Trails located in a conservation area or a provincial/national park often have special events and interpretive centres, and may involve a modest admission, parking or participation fee. Some areas are closed during the off-season, while others allow seasonal uses such as snowmobiling and hunting. It's best to call ahead.

When an area is closed, hiking is often permitted, but facilities aren't available. If a conservation area allows hunting in spring or fall, wear a safety vest or brightly coloured clothing. You may prefer to visit at another time of year.

Environmental Ethics

Since these trails are primarily for the enjoyment of nature, including fragile plants, there is a protocol to observe. Trampling vegetation along the edges of a trail can alter the habitat; some plants take years to grow back. Proceed directly through wet, muddy spots. Also, don't deliberately make noise to spook animals; they need their energy to search for food.

Pets should be leashed. Dogs can chase wildlife, harm ground-nesting songbirds and transfer poison ivy to owners.

Safety Notes

There are inherent risks in travelling on foot through natural areas. On escarpment properties, many trails edge the escarpment and there are no fences to guard against steep slopes. Some crevices, starting right at the edge of the trail, are hidden by pine trees and bushes.

Depending on weather and time of the year, some trail surfaces near the water can be muddy or icy. Limestone can also be dangerous and slippery when wet.

Poison ivy takes many forms and is quite rampant off the maintained trail areas. Look for three shiny leaflets on a single stem with the middle leaf having a longer stalk.

Some trails are in remote locations. Lock all valuables in the trunk of your car to ensure the safety of your belongings.

Trail Etiquette

Referred to as "multi-use trails," many paths might be shared by hikers, mountain bikers, equestrians and joggers. Following are some trail etiquette guidelines:

- Stay to the right and allow other users room to pass on your left. For example, joggers and cyclists should avoid travelling in "packs."
- Yield to pedestrians; they have the right of way on multi-use trails.
- If you are cycling and passing other trail users, sound your bell or call out ("On your left") and then pass safely on the user's left side. Be especially cautious when approaching horseback riders, children or dogs from the rear.

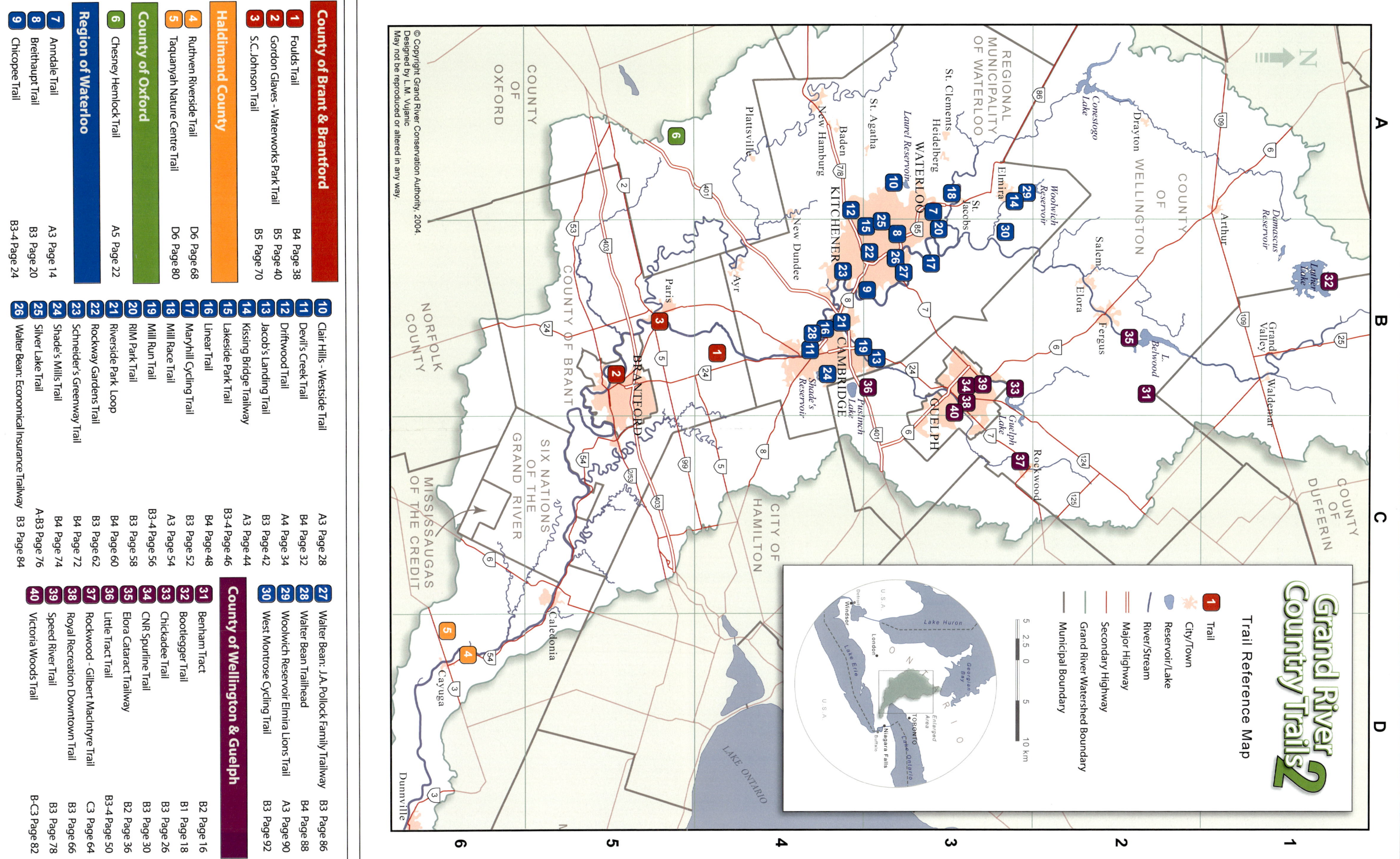

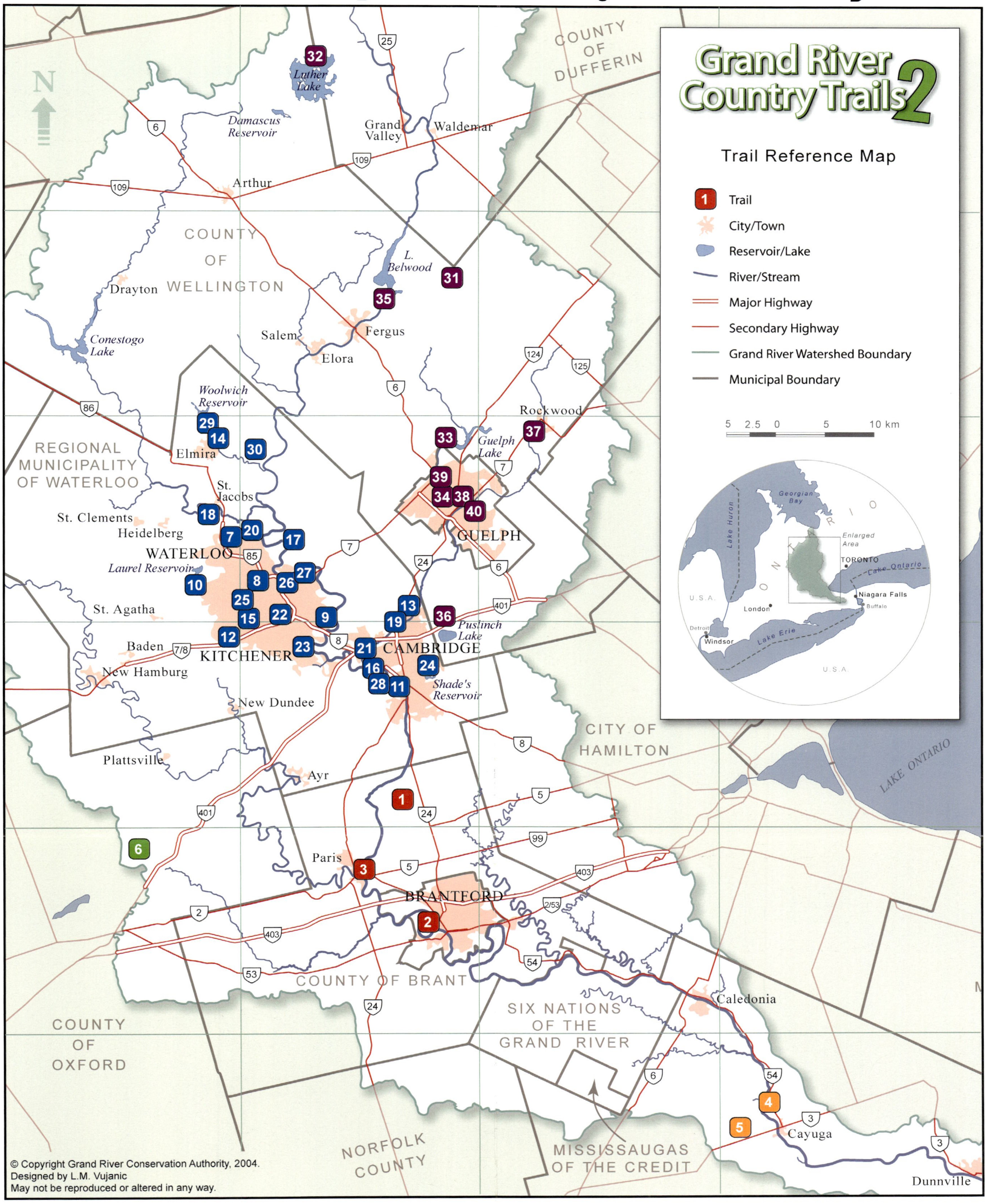
Grand River Country Trails 2
Trail Reference Map
Trail
City/Town
Reservoir/Lake
River/Stream
Major Highway
Secondary Highway
Grand River Watershed Boundary
Municipal Boundary
5 2.5 0 5 10 km
A
B
C
D
1
2
3
4
5
6
N
COUNTY OF WELLINGTON
COUNTY OF DUFFERIN
REGIONAL MUNICIPALITY OF WATERLOO
CITY OF HAMILTON
COUNTY OF BRANT
COUNTY OF OXFORD
SIX NATIONS OF THE GRAND RIVER
MISSISSAUGAS OF THE CREDIT
NORFOLK COUNTY
LAKE ONTARIO
Luther Lake
Damascus Reservoir
Grand Valley
Waldemar
Arthur
L. Belwood
Drayton
Conestogo Lake
Salem
Fergus
Elora
Woolwich Reservoir
Rockwood
Elmira
Guelph Lake
St. Jacobs
St. Clements
Heidelberg
GUELPH
WATERLOO
Laurel Reservoir
St. Agatha
Puslinch Lake
Baden
KITCHENER
CAMBRIDGE
New Hamburg
Shade's Reservoir
New Dundee
Plattsville
Ayr
Paris
BRANTFORD
Caledonia
Cayuga
Dunnville
Lake Huron
Georgian Bay
O N T A R I O
Enlarged Area
TORONTO
Lake Ontario
Niagara Falls
Buffalo
London
Detroit
Windsor
Lake Erie
U.S.A.
U.S.A.
© Copyright Grand River Conservation Authority, 2004.
Designed by L.M. Vujanic
May not be reproduced or altered in any way.

County of Brant & Brantford

1	Foulds Trail	B4 Page 38
2	Gordon Glaves - Waterworks Park Trail	B5 Page 40
3	S.C. Johnson Trail	B5 Page 70

Haldimand County

4	Ruthven Riverside Trail	D6 Page 68
5	Taquanyah Nature Centre Trail	D6 Page 80

County of Oxford

6	Chesney Hemlock Trail	A5 Page 22

Region of Waterloo

7	Anndale Trail	A3 Page 14
8	Breithaupt Trail	B3 Page 20
9	Chicopee Trail	B3-4 Page 24
10	Clair Hills - Westside Trail	A3 Page 28
11	Devil's Creek Trail	B4 Page 32
12	Driftwood Trail	A4 Page 34
13	Jacob's Landing Trail	B3 Page 42
14	Kissing Bridge Trailway	A3 Page 44
15	Lakeside Park Trail	B3-4 Page 46
16	Linear Trail	B4 Page 48
17	Maryhill Cycling Trail	B3 Page 52
18	Mill Race Trail	A3 Page 54
19	Mill Run Trail	B3-4 Page 56
20	RIM Park Trail	B3 Page 58
21	Riverside Park Loop	B4 Page 60
22	Rockway Gardens Trail	B3 Page 62
23	Schneider's Greenway Trail	B4 Page 72
24	Shade's Mills Trail	B4 Page 74
25	Silver Lake Trail	A-B3 Page 76
26	Walter Bean: Economical Insurance Trailway	B3 Page 84
27	Walter Bean: J.A. Pollock Family Trailway	B3 Page 86
28	Walter Bean Trailhead	B4 Page 88
29	Woolwich Reservoir Elmira Lions Trail	A3 Page 90
30	West Montrose Cycling Trail	B3 Page 92

County of Wellington & Guelph

31	Benham Tract	B2 Page 16
32	Bootlegger Trail	B1 Page 18
33	Chickadee Trail	B3 Page 26
34	CNR Spurline Trail	B3 Page 30
35	Elora Cataract Trailway	B2 Page 36
36	Little Tract Trail	B3-4 Page 50
37	Rockwood - Gilbert MacIntyre Trail	C3 Page 64
38	Royal Recreation Downtown Trail	B3 Page 66
39	Speed River Trail	B3 Page 78
40	Victoria Woods Trail	B-C3 Page 82

Anndale Trail, Waterloo

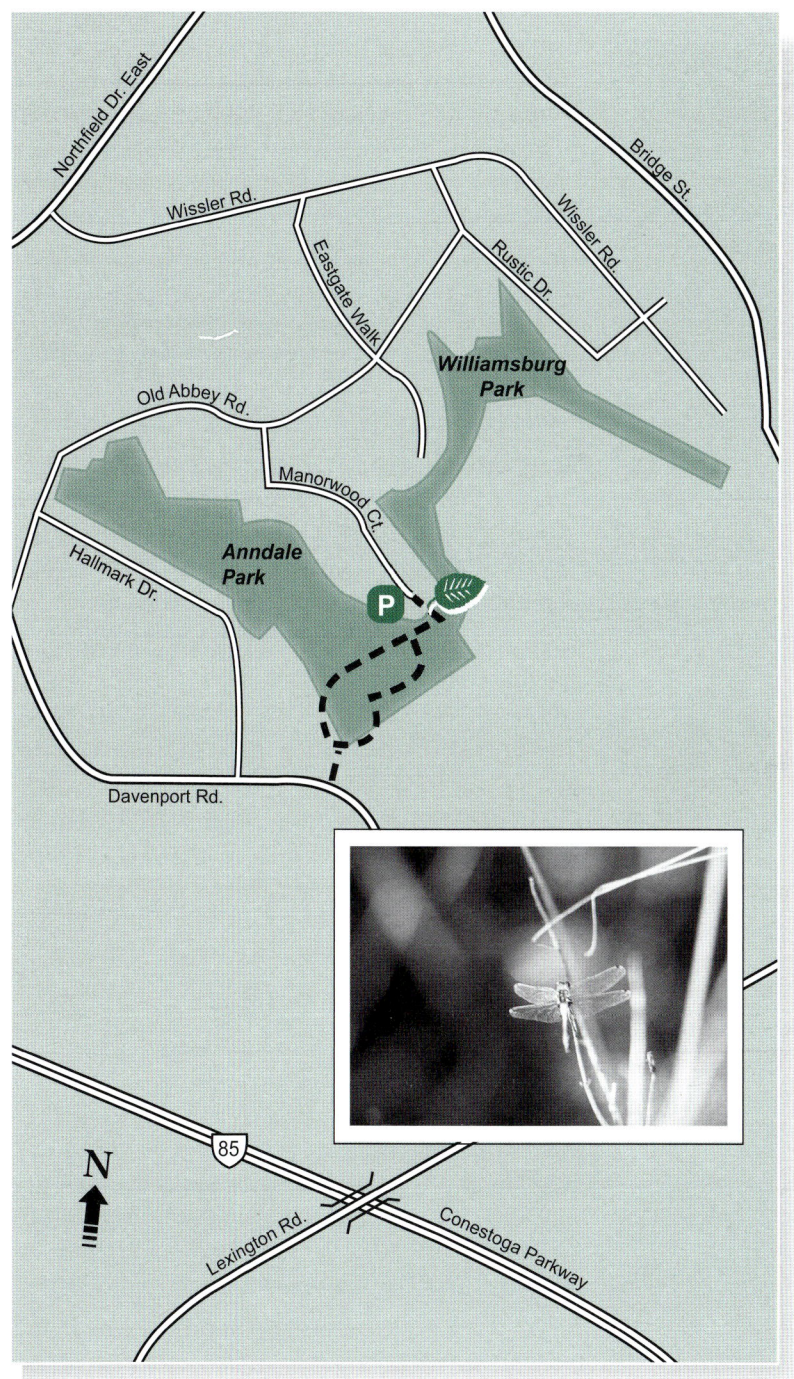

Benham Tract, Fergus

- 3 km linear
- Beginner

This is one of the best trails in Wellington County -- diverse and quiet. Part of the reason is the location. Often, getting to a trail involves traveling along city streets, close to development and traffic noise. However, getting to the Benham Tract involves driving on a gravel road -- truly in the country.

The long, wide pathway leads through evergreens where pine boughs reach their arms toward the trail and touch each other. The pine trees are taller than in most plantations and you actually have to crane your neck to follow them toward the sky. The bottom branches are bare of needles, allowing a deeper view into the forest.

When the main pathway reaches a T-intersection, the trail changes. Turn right and the side trail narrows into a thick cedar grove, which can be wet in the spring. As the cedars end, so does this pathway at a private property sign. Please respect that boundary.

Turn left at the T-intersection and the side trail becomes rugged, climbing a steep hill into a hardwood forest. At the top, you can turn 360 degrees and see deep into the valleys and rolling hills below you.

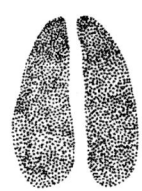

Look for deer tracks along this trail

From here you can choose more than three different trails for your descent. These side trails wind down hills and valleys, around switchbacks and eventually return on a straighter path a few meters away from the tranquil one you started on. Make sure you look for deer tracks along this trail. They have regular passageways to the creek that flows through the forest.

TRAIL SURFACE: Hard-packed earth.

IF YOU GO: From Highway 401, take the Hanlon Expressway/Highway 6 North to Guelph. Turn right on Wellington Road 124 (Old Highway 24) through Guelph. Just east of Brucedale, turn north (left) on Eramosa 7th Line. (Wellington Road 49 goes in the opposite direction.) Just north of Sideroad 30, look for the trail on your right-hand side next to a faded yellow MNR sign. If you reach the Eramosa-Garafraxa Townline, you've gone too far.

Benham Tract, Fergus

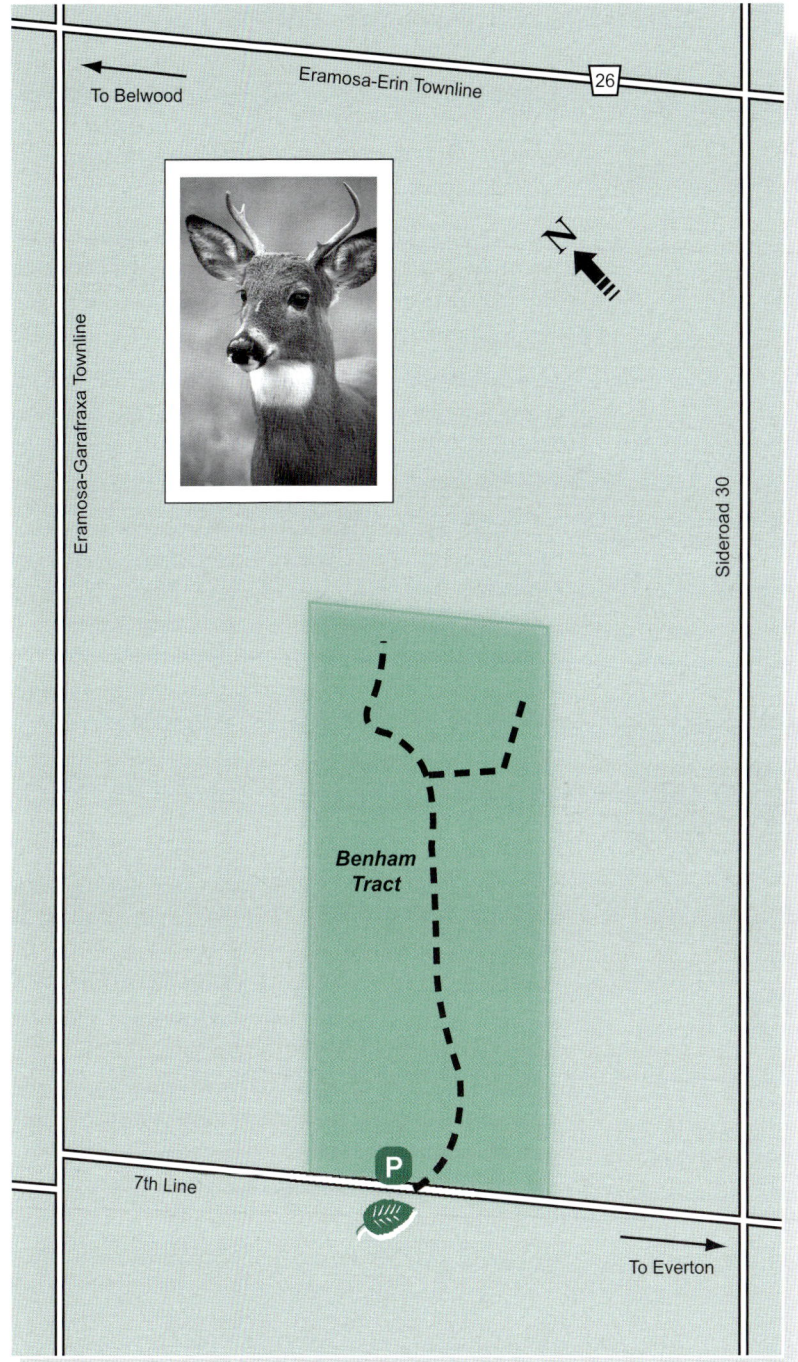

To Belwood

Eramosa-Erin Townline 26

Eramosa-Garafraxa Townline

N

Sideroad 30

Benham
Tract

7th Line

P

To Everton

Bootlegger Trail - Luther Marsh Wildlife Management Area, Grand Valley

- 15 km linear

- Beginner

The trail follows a level gravel interior road along the shore of Luther Lake, a 1,400 hectare (3,500 acre) shallow, marshy lake containing numerous islands and surrounded by an extensive low shrub bog.

From the dam, it's a 9 km cycle to Bootlegger Bay, an ideal place to spot grebes, coots and blue-winged teal. Look closely for damselflies darting among the plants. If you cycle another 6 km you'll reach the south end of the lake.

Midway to Bootlegger, stop at a path that leads to a small pond. In the soil you may see the footprints of raccoons or the broken shells of turtle eggs. These are all inhabitants of Luther, along with the waterfowl.

Luther Marsh is one of the largest inland marshes in Ontario and a summer breeding ground for many species, including the provincially rare redhead, least bittern and great egret. It's also an important migration stopover for shore birds. The marsh has four wetland types (bog, marsh, swamp, and fen meadows) that are not normally found together in one area. Wetlands are important to Ontario, one of their prime functions being to slow and sustain local water flow.

One of the largest inland marshes in Ontario

TRAIL SURFACE: Gravel.

IF YOU GO: From Highway 401 take the Hanlon Expressway/Highway 6 North through Guelph and Fergus to Arthur. Turn right on County Road 109 (former Highway 9) and then left on Dufferin Road 25 through Grand Valley. Turn west (left) on East Luther Township Sideroad 6-7. Follow this sideroad to the end, then turn right and follow the signs to the main Luther Marsh Wildlife Management Area entrance (phone 519-928-2832). The parking area is on your left, and a modest self-registration fee applies. During hunting season (approximately mid-September to year-end), hiking is restricted to Tuesdays, Thursdays and Sundays.

Bootlegger Trail - Luther Marsh Wildlife Management Area, Grand Valley

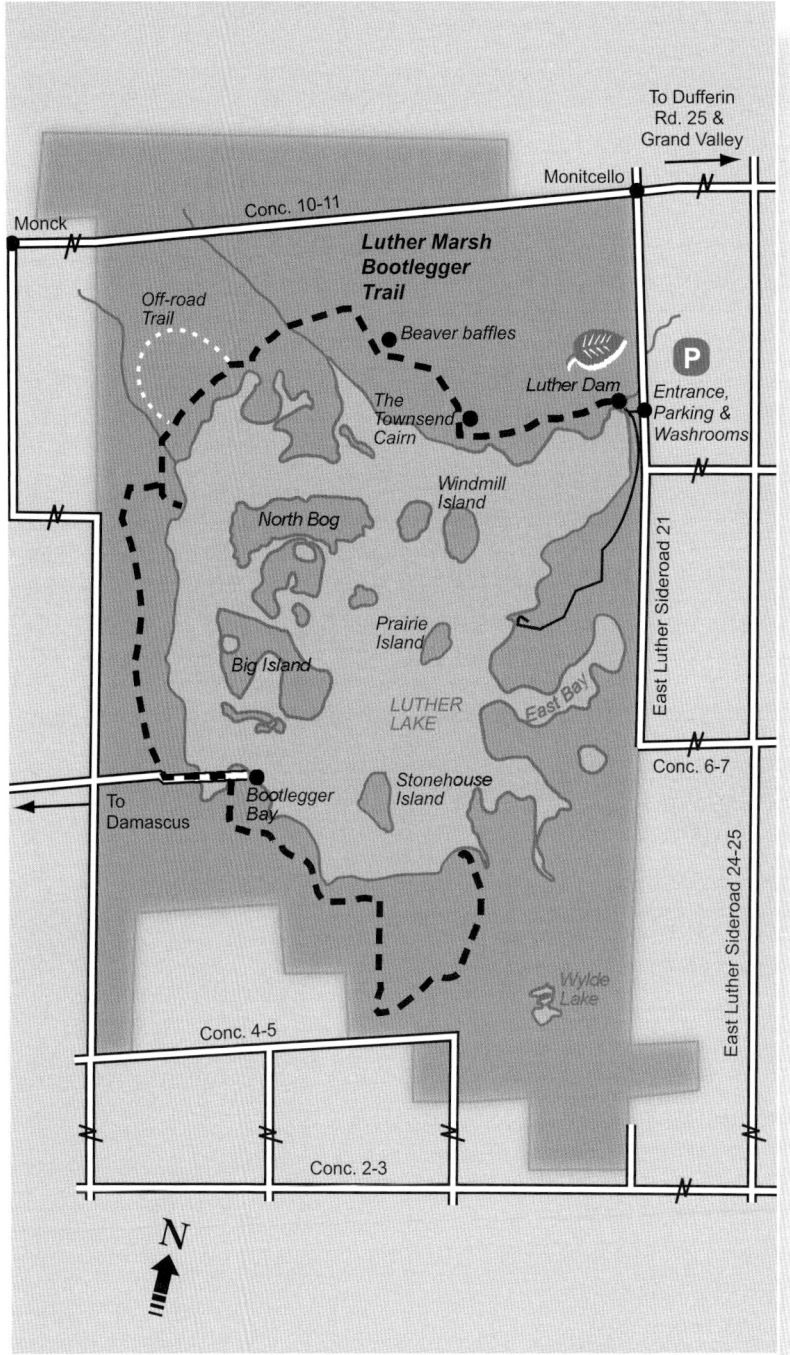

Breithaupt Trail, Kitchener

- 1.4 km loop

- Beginner

Many trails in our region run through hardwood forests, but few have trees that are centuries old. This is the unique part of the Breithaupt Bush. The remains of a climax forest are sprinkled throughout this woodland's rolling hills. Some sugar maple and beech trees are fairly large, and near the picnic shelter at the Union Street entrance stand three large red oak trees, each more than 250 years old.

Although much attention is focused on the baseball fields and the Breithaupt Centre itself, the bush across the street has a loop trail that winds through hills and valleys. The pathway starts from the right of the playground and loops in the forest bordering Maplewood Place and the Conestoga Parkway. There's a second entrance on the expressway wall along Edwin Street.

There are secondary trails through Breithaupt Bush, but stay on the existing trails as certain areas have been closed where trampling, soil erosion and compaction prevent regeneration. The city is taking great efforts to expand the woodland edges through natural regeneration and planting. Fallen limbs and trunks are also being left to rot, in order to replenish the nutrients in the soil. Please leave this woodland untouched.

If you want to walk a longer trail, there is another loop toward Margaret Avenue, but with the rolling hills in this bush, it does take longer to complete the trail.

Three large red oak trees, each more than 250 years old

TRAIL SURFACE: Hard-packed earth.

IF YOU GO: From the Conestoga Parkway, take the Bridgeport Road exit. Travel west/right on Bridgeport Road. Turn left on Margaret Avenue and turn left onto Union Street. You'll see a Breithaupt Park sign and parking lot near a playground area. The trail starts there.

Breithaupt Trail, Kitchener

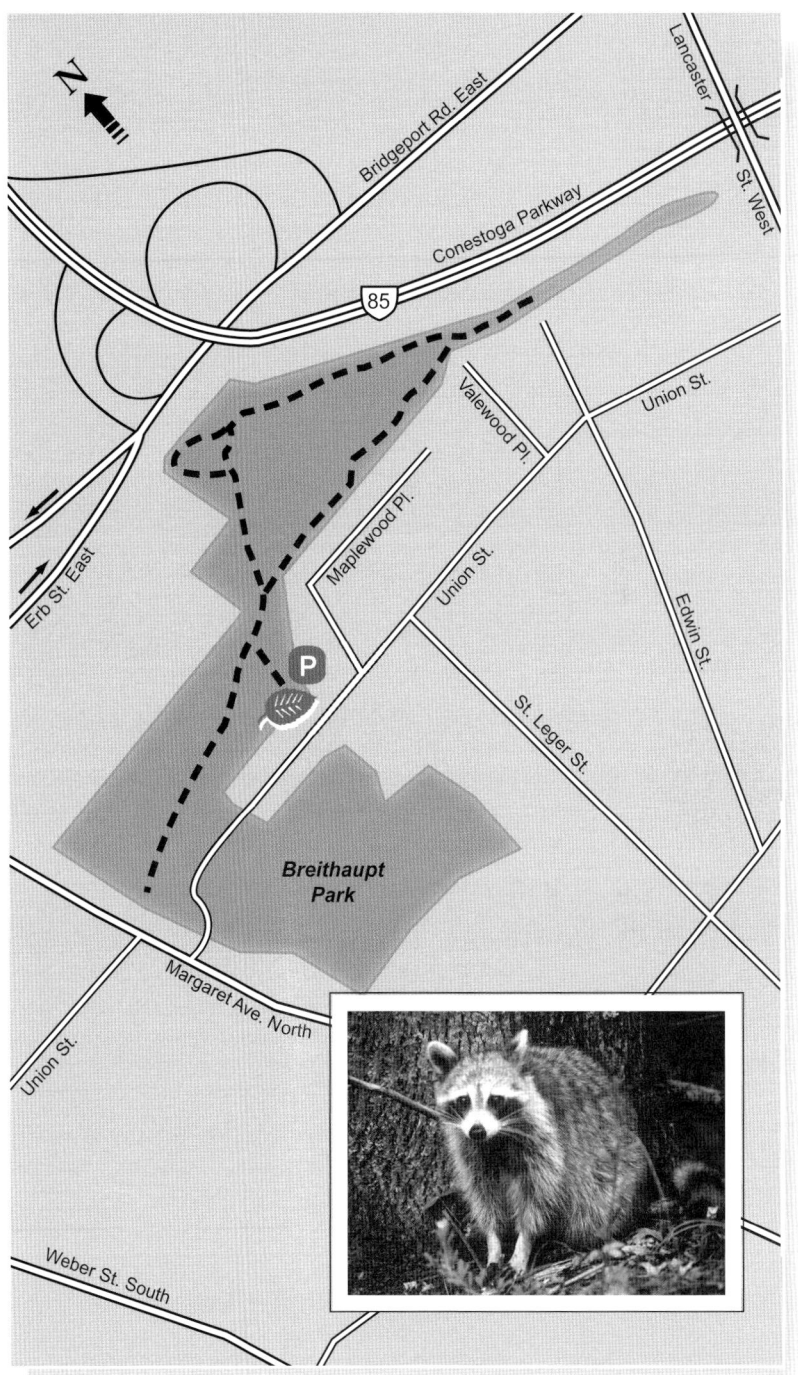

Chesney Hemlock Trail, Drumbo

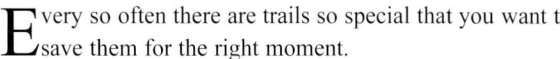

- 2 km loop
- Beginner

Every so often there are trails so special that you want to save them for the right moment.

Start down the Maple Trail where tree branches reach into the long laneway. The pathway narrows in the pine plantation before opening to a forest filled with large hardwoods. This is the Hemlock Trail, which peers onto colours in the valley below. The pathway climbs and dips through the valley and then wraps around the hillside.

Does it seem as if the forest is floating? As if you can see through it? This is the softness of hemlock. Compare it to the solid green of the cedars and you'll see the difference.

There aren't many trails in this region where you'll find a large section of hemlocks along a trail. And these hemlocks are large. It's the special part along this trail.

Linger. Stare long enough until you can see through the forest.

When you are ready to carry on, you'll pass through a cedar swamp with a long boardwalk. When you come out of the boardwalk area you'll continue through cedars, on a path so narrow that only one person can walk through at a time. Stay to the left to complete the loop. You'll return on the Maple Trail. Catch a maple leaf as it's drifting toward you in the wind…it may remind you of the hemlock forest, floating in the valley.

*Linger.
Stare long
enough until you
can see through
the forest*

TRAIL SURFACE: Hard packed earth.

IF YOU GO: Take Highway 401 toward London and take Exit 250, Oxford Road 29, Drumbo/Innerkip. Turn west/right on Drumbo Road toward Innerkip. After passing Oxford County Road 22, look for the Conservation Area sign on your right. There is a large parking lot.

Chesney Hemlock Trail, Drumbo

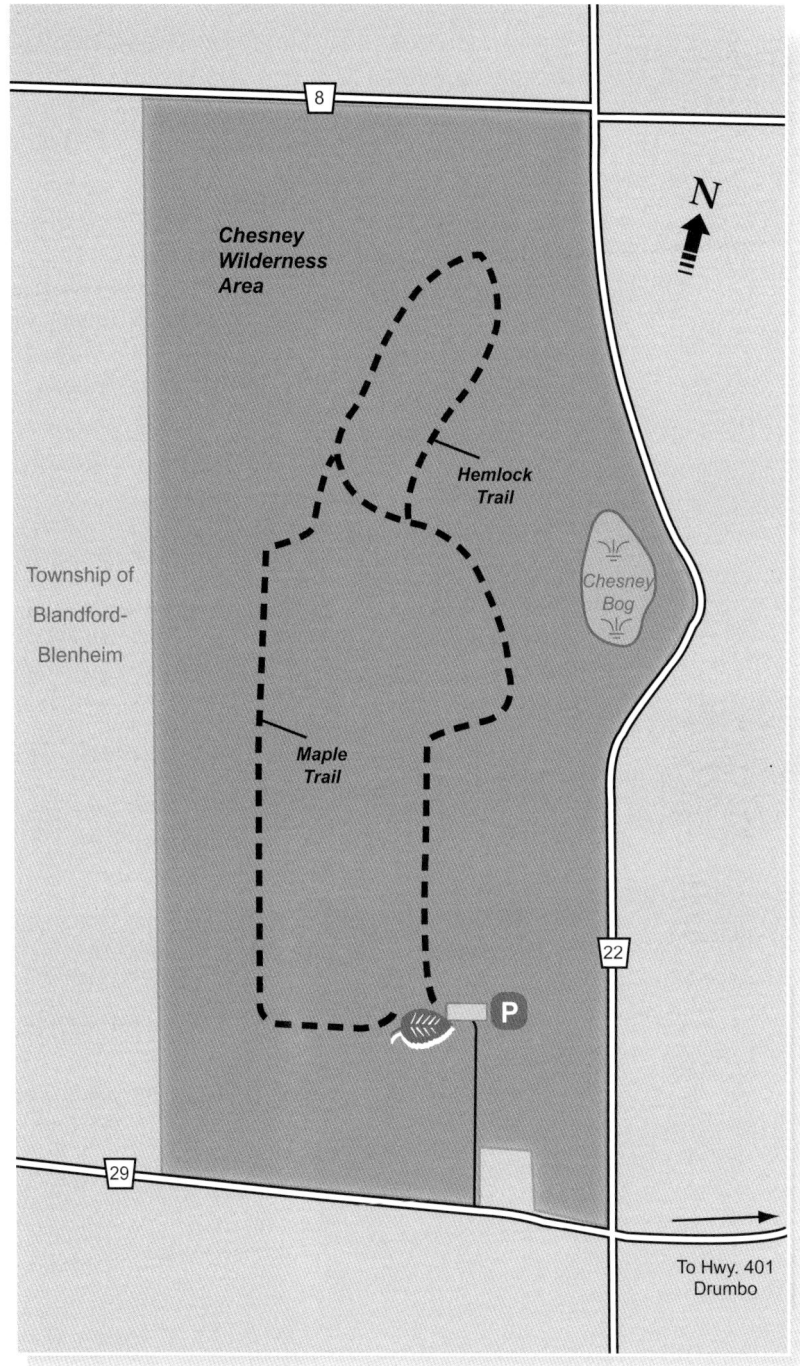

Chicopee Trail, Kitchener

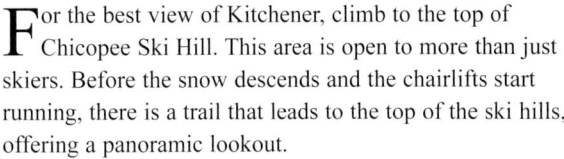

- 2.6 km linear
- Beginner

For the best view of Kitchener, climb to the top of Chicopee Ski Hill. This area is open to more than just skiers. Before the snow descends and the chairlifts start running, there is a trail that leads to the top of the ski hills, offering a panoramic lookout.

From the parking lot, walk past the chalet and into parking lot B to view the pond area where you'll see many birds among the bulrushes. Then follow the roadway, which wraps around the base of the ski hills. You'll pass the maintenance facility and then reach a small wetland area on your left. The tall, dark purple plumes that rise from this area are canary reed grass.

From this point, the trail starts climbing upwards. Some sections are steep, but the views from the top are worth every step. As you ascend the hill, there are small pathways that veer from the main trail. Each takes you to the top.

The trail climbs to the summit. At 373 metres (1,223 feet), it offers a panoramic view of the city. When you've taken in the sights, you can walk near the chairlift and go down North, Micmac or any of the other surrounding hills.

Before walking to the summit, the trail comes out at North Hill Place and Fairway Road. From here you can continue on a trail along Scenic Drive or head into the Stanley Park trail system.

TRAIL SURFACE: Hard-packed earth.

IF YOU GO: From Kitchener, take King Street East toward the Grand River and turn left on Morrison Road. After crossing Grand River Boulevard, pass the Chicopee Ski Club South Parking Lot and park in the main skiing area parking lot.

For the best view of Kitchener, climb to the top of Chicopee Ski Hill

Chicopee Trail, Kitchener

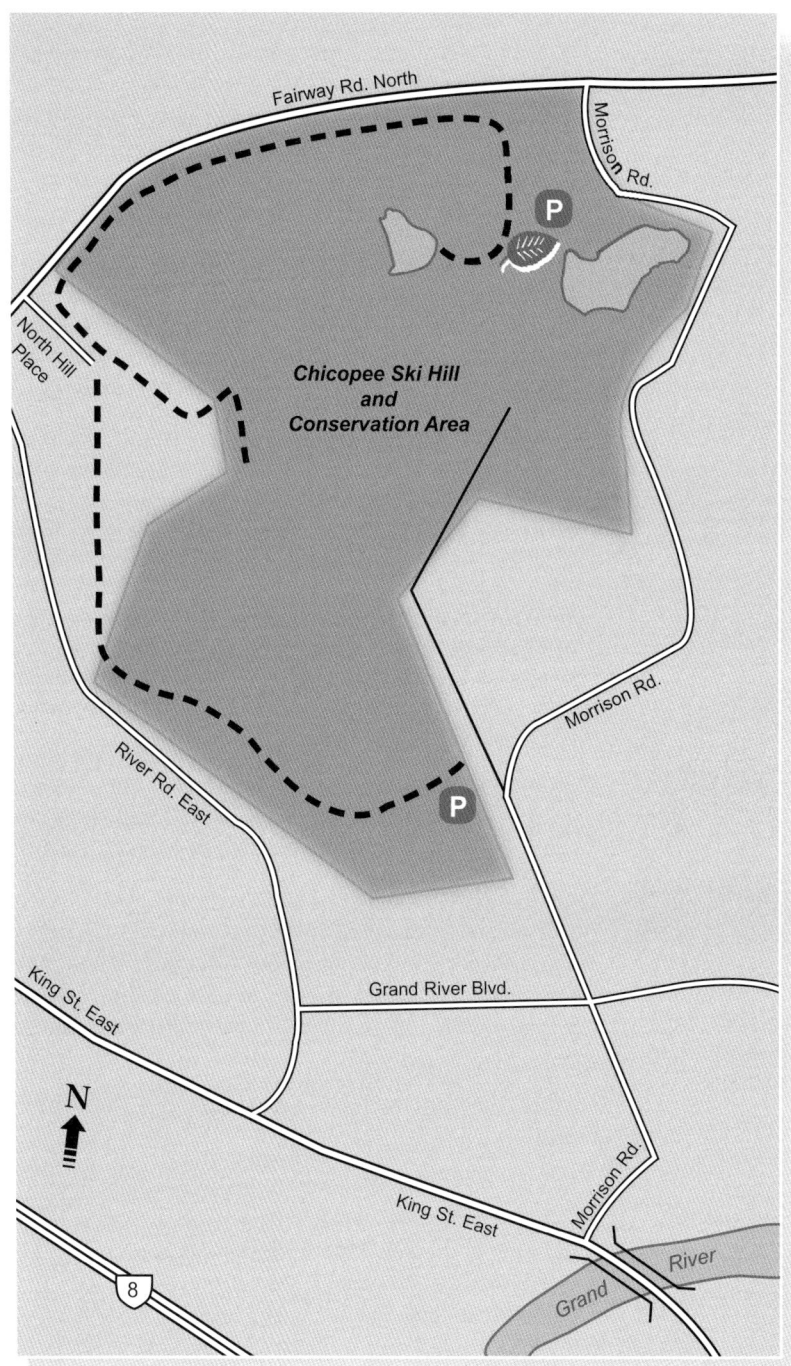

Chickadee Trail, Guelph Lake

- **1.5 km loop**
- **Beginner**

Even when there's no snow on the ground, there can still be signs of winter. One is the black-capped chickadee, the bold, inquisitive birds of winter. Even on a blustery cold winter day, their bubbly "chicka-dee-dee-dee" rings in forests. In backyards their tiny beaks lightly tap against birdfeeders as they crack open sunflower seeds.

Listen for their call as you begin exploring around the Guelph Lake Nature Centre building. Pass the willow trees and head into the coniferous forest. As you near the first large bend you'll spot small fluffy bodies with white cheeks and black caps fluttering to the feeder, picking seeds and then darting off.

One of the chickadee's main reasons for winter survival is its food storage capability. They have been known to store up to a thousand seeds in a single day, and northern populations store even more food. Chickadees can even remember where they have already removed stored seeds.

Wide sweeping views of Guelph Lake accompany you on the return portion of this trail. You'll cross a boardwalk, pass a pond and a few side trails that lead to the lake edge. There are many smaller loop trails through the forest and longer sections that lead along the entire lake.

If you linger near the feeder, the birds will eat seeds right out of your hand. When your palm is empty they may search your hat, your hair, or even pick at your ears to find hidden seeds.

Take off your mitts to feel this bird land on your hand

It is a powerful moment that such a tiny bird can give you. Take off your mitts to feel this bird land on your hand and wrap its tiny claws around your finger. It is a moment of trust. Wild and human. Cold and warm. Feather and skin. In this brief instant, you may catch its eye, and feel as vulnerable as the chickadee...and as free.

TRAIL SURFACE: Hard-packed earth with rocks and grass.

IF YOU GO: From Highway 401, take the Hanlon Expressway/Highway 6 North toward Guelph. Turn right on Highway 24 traveling through the city and then left on Wellington Road 38/Victoria Road. Turn right on Conservation Road and park at the Nature Centre. Phone (519) 836-7860 for hours of operation and family hike program information.

Chickadee Trail, Guelph Lake

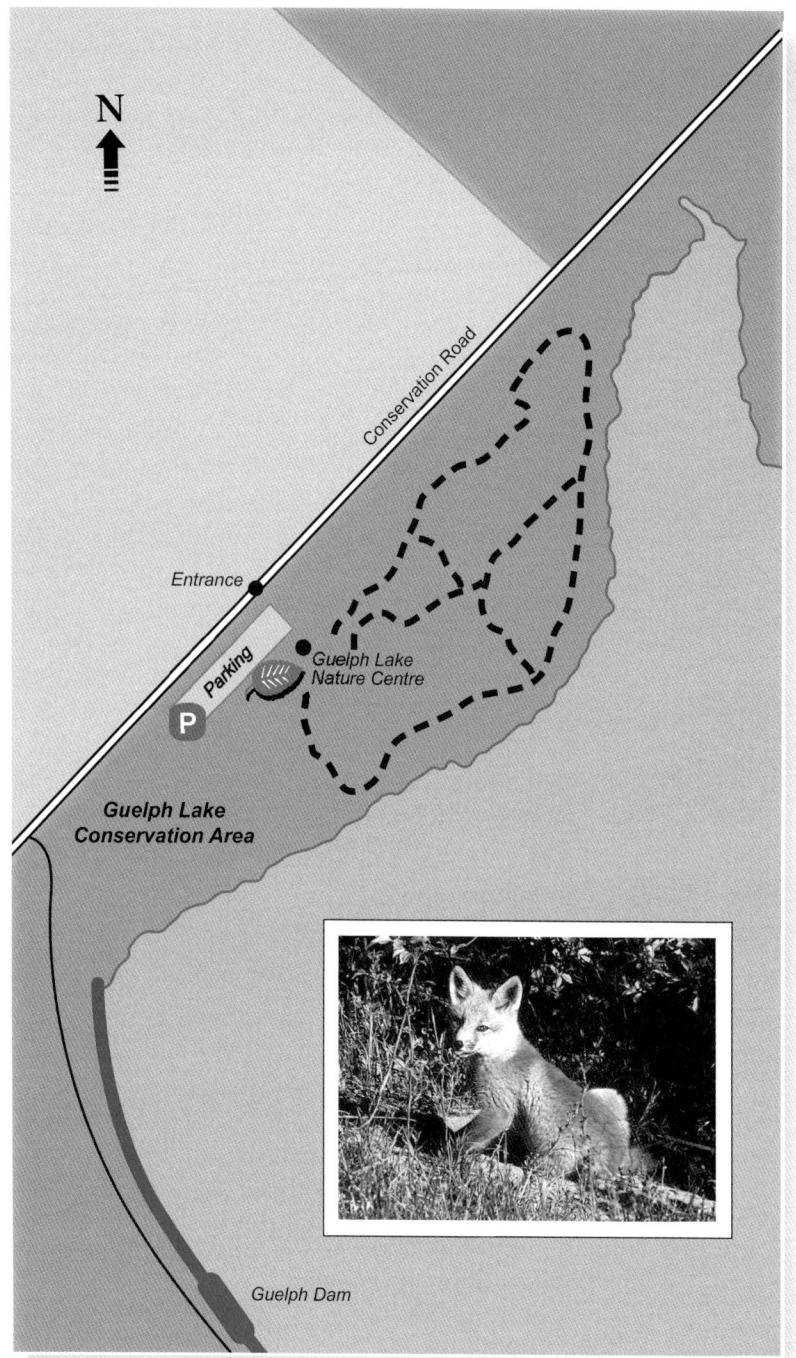

N

Conservation Road

Entrance

Parking

P

Guelph Lake
Nature Centre

Guelph Lake
Conservation Area

Guelph Dam

Clair Hills - Westside Trail, Waterloo

- 4 km linear
- Intermediate

Imagine an area as far as your eye can see, covered in ice. It happened in our watershed more than 23,000 years ago, and there are still remnants of this glacial period in the high ridges of sand and gravel that were deposited when the massive ice sheet retreated.

If you want to get a feel for how this area looked, walk the Clair Hills section of the Westside Trail during the winter. With snow covering the ground and rooftops of the nearby subdivision in white, the path leads to a vantage point on the edge of the Waterloo moraine, where 14,000 years ago a huge ice sheet would have extended far to the east and north.

The trail starts off skirting the environmentally protected forest with the subdivision to your left. When you reach the top of the hill, an illustrated panel explains the formation and importance of the Waterloo moraine in more detail. Press the audio sign on the right-hand side of the panel and then take a seat on the bench to listen to more information. It's the first audio panel on a trail in our region.

When you continue on the trail, don't go down the hill to your right. Instead take the trail to the left that leads into the forest. You will loop through the forest and reach another interesting audio panel about kettle lakes. When you enter the main trail bordering the subdivision, turn left to complete the loop.

Hike to a vantage point on the edge of the Waterloo moraine

The Waterloo moraine is an important storage area for groundwater reserves and provides drinking water for Kitchener, Waterloo and Cambridge.

TRAIL SURFACE: Hard-packed earth and stone dust, some steep areas.

IF YOU GO: From the Conestoga Parkway, take the University Avenue West exit. Continue on University then turn right onto Weber Street, then left onto Columbia Street. After crossing Erbsville Road, turn right on Salzburg, left on Munich Crossing and right onto Munich Circle. Park on the street near the trail gate by the mailboxes.

Clair Hills - Westside Trail, Waterloo

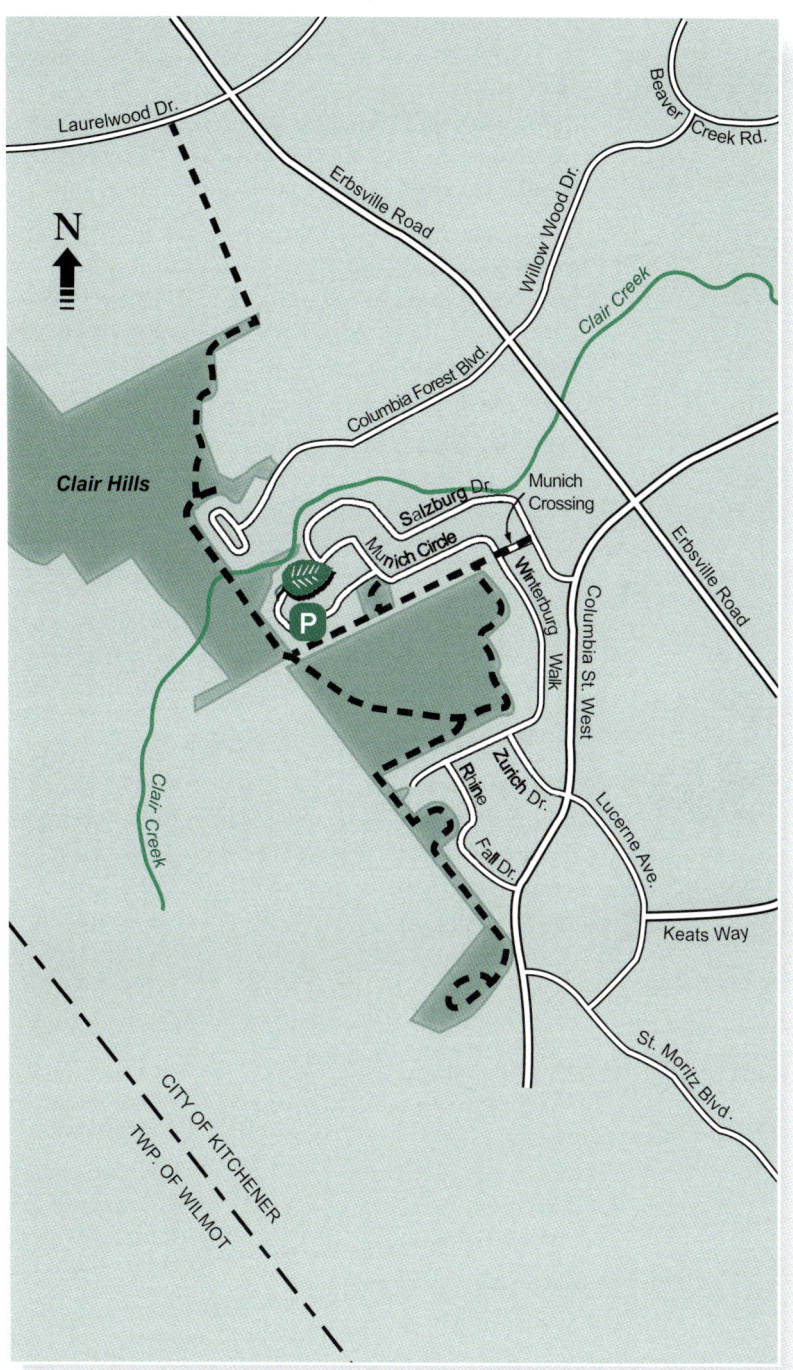

CNR Spurline Trail, Guelph

- 1.6 km linear
- Beginner

For a bit of green close to the downtown core, follow the C.N.R. Spurline Trail, tucked in behind ridges and forested corridors. You'll see the Royal Recreation Trail sign behind the plaza. From here, the pathway follows a small green space that leads through a residential area.

Your marker for a good portion of the trail is the City of Guelph water tower that you walk toward after crossing Westmount. The trail eventually leads to Exhibition Park. Other than the arena, the park is fairly quiet during the winter, allowing you to stroll and look for the tracks of animal that have passed through the wide, open space the night before.

The trail eventually ends near the Speed River. Follow it down to the water's edge for a peaceful moment. You'll see waterfowl swimming in the open areas: Canada geese, mallards and perhaps even some early migrating ducks such as a hooded merganser, wood duck or American widgeon.

This trail is part of the Royal Recreation Trail System that leads throughout Guelph. You can connect with other trails that follow the Speed River.

TRAIL SURFACE: Hard-packed earth, gravel and grass.

IF YOU GO: From the Hanlon Expressway (Highway 6) travel east (toward downtown) on Paisley Road. Turn left on Edinburgh Road and right on London Road. Park along Hamel Avenue or in the park off Kathleen and Exhibition Streets.

Look for the tracks of animals that have passed the night before

CNR Spurline Trail, Guelph

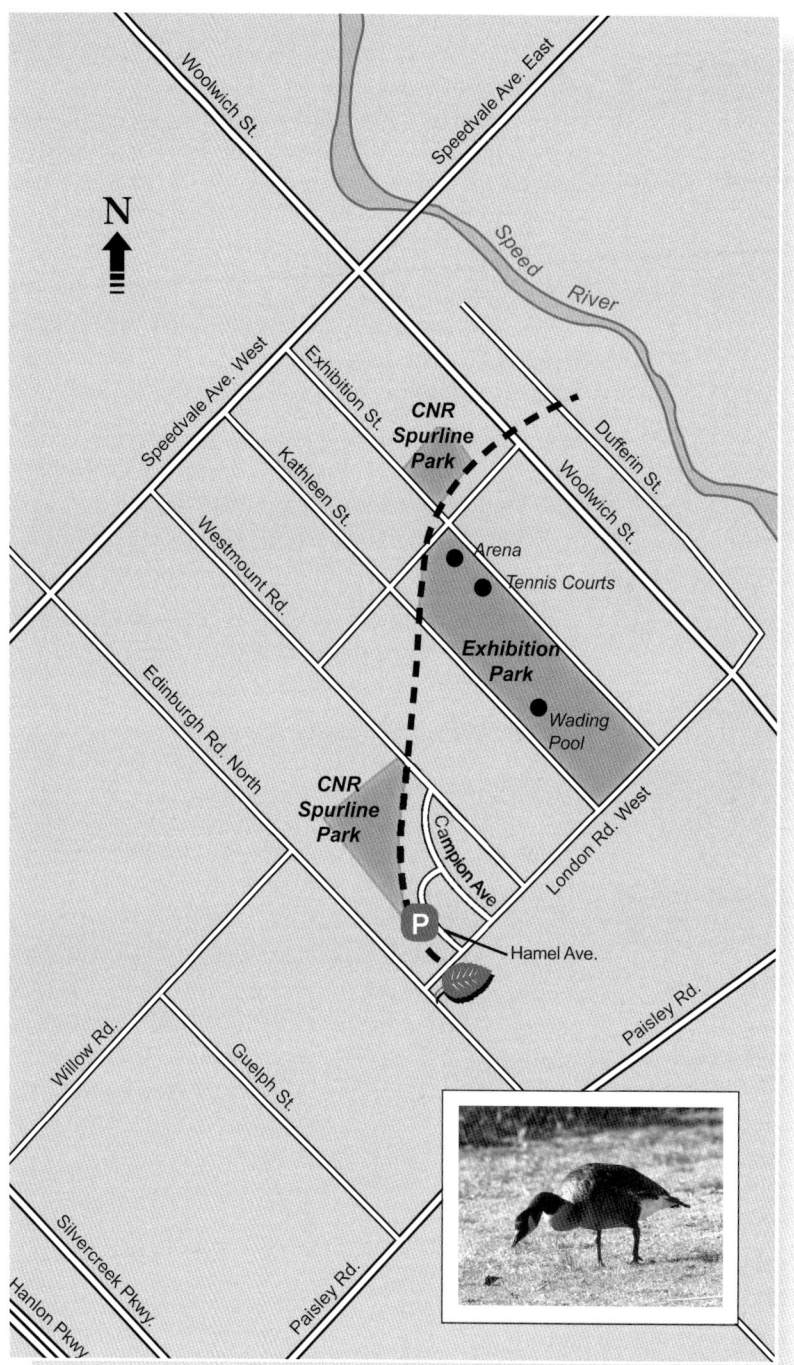

N

Woolwich St.

Speedvale Ave. East

Speed River

Speedvale Ave. West

Exhibition St.

Kathleen St.

CNR Spurline Park

Westmount Rd.

Dufferin St.

Woolwich St.

● Arena

● Tennis Courts

Exhibition Park

● Wading Pool

Edinburgh Rd. North

CNR Spurline Park

Campion Ave

London Rd. West

P

Hamel Ave.

Paisley Rd.

Willow Rd.

Guelph St.

Silvercreek Pkwy.

Hanlon Pkwy

Paisley Rd.

Devil's Creek Trail, Cambridge

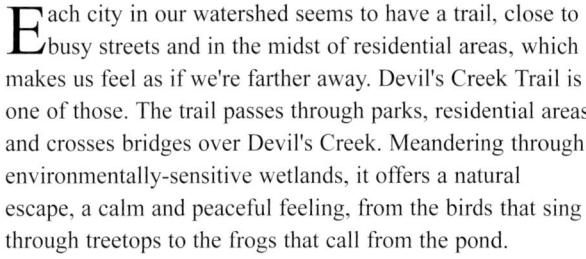

- 3 km linear

- Beginner

Each city in our watershed seems to have a trail, close to busy streets and in the midst of residential areas, which makes us feel as if we're farther away. Devil's Creek Trail is one of those. The trail passes through parks, residential areas and crosses bridges over Devil's Creek. Meandering through environmentally-sensitive wetlands, it offers a natural escape, a calm and peaceful feeling, from the birds that sing through treetops to the frogs that call from the pond.

It's the creek that is your constant companion on the trail, bubbling along its course and pausing in wider channels. Stop on the bridge to listen to the sounds.

Interpretive signs explain the naturalization efforts to restore this creek, such as a wetland pool created for amphibian breeding habitats. Located next to the trail, an interpretive sign explains the naturalization work.

Along the trail you'll find more panels providing information about wetlands and stream life. After crossing the boardwalk under the railway, the trail winds through woods and takes you farther away from city sights and sounds.

On your return, cross over Blair Road to continue on this trail through Morva Rouse Parkette. If you want a longer walk, this trail connects with the 7.5 km stone dust and asphalt Grand Trunk Trail. You'll see the Devil's Creek waterfall and the heart-shaped Galt Fossil in the limestone bluffs.

*Frogs call
from the pond*

TRAIL SURFACE: Stone dust, boardwalk.

IF YOU GO: From Highway 401 and Kitchener, take Highway 8 south toward Cambridge. Turn right on Fountain Street and left on Waterloo Regional Road 42. After driving through the village of Blair and countryside, take the right fork to Blair Street when you come to the fork in the road (left takes you to George Street). You'll see a parking lot on your right hand side.

Devil's Creek Trail, Cambridge

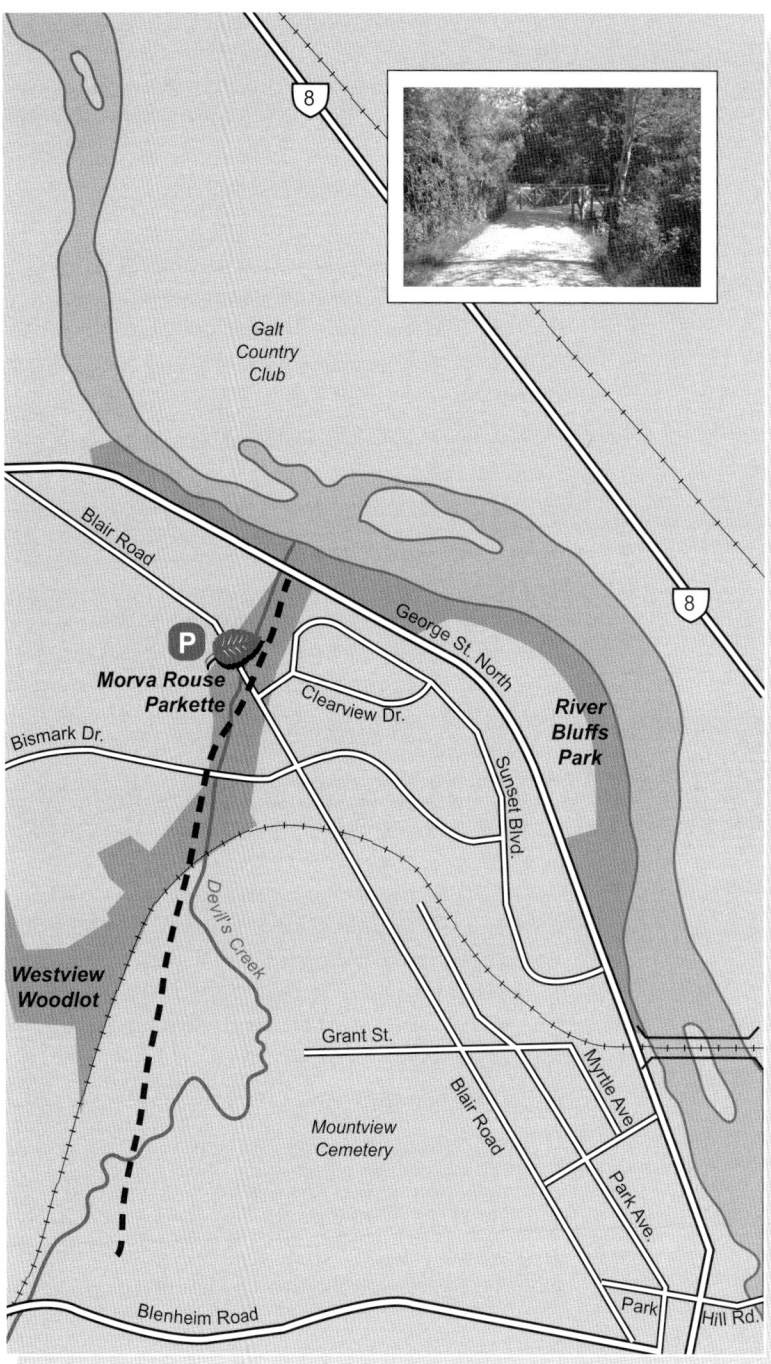

Driftwood Trail, Kitchener

- 8 km loop
- Beginner

Whenever hydro poles are used as trail markers instead of natural features, it's indicative of how little nature is left in the city core. There are, however, little pockets of green and open spaces and the Driftwood Trail, although surrounded by houses, is connected to Meadowlane and Driftwood Park.

In the wintertime, you don't need to follow trail markers other than the actual tracks in the snow left by previous walkers. This trail is well used, but you must be careful to stay on the main trail and not follow side routes that lead into smaller subdivisions.

From the mall, head toward the hydro poles and start on the trail that follows them. You'll cross over Royal Orchard Drive where you'll hear screams of delight from children as they toboggan down the hill.

From here the trail leaves the hydro poles, rounds a corner and parallels the Conestoga Parkway. The traffic noise fades somewhat when you go down a hill into a wooded area. Although there are cross-country skiing tracks, they are quite obscured as the snow has a crusty layer and depressions from boots create an uneven skiing surface.

Tracks in the snow left by previous walkers mark the trail

The trail eventually circles to meet up with the hydro poles again. You'll follow a road and pick up the trail by the hydro poles. You'll cross over Yellow Birch Drive and Highview Drive and reach a main intersection of hydro poles. At this junction, stay to the right and continue up the hill. The tracks will disappear due to drifting snow, but this trail eventually reaches Driftwood Drive. Remember that Driftwood is a crescent and you must wait till the second street crossing before turning left at the church.

TRAIL SURFACE: Gravel.

IF YOU GO: From the Conestoga Parkway, take the Fischer-Hallman Road exit. Go north on Fischer-Hallman and turn left onto McGarry Drive. Turn left onto Westheights Drive and left onto Driftwood Drive. Park in the Westheights Mall or along the main streets.

Driftwood Trail, Kitchener

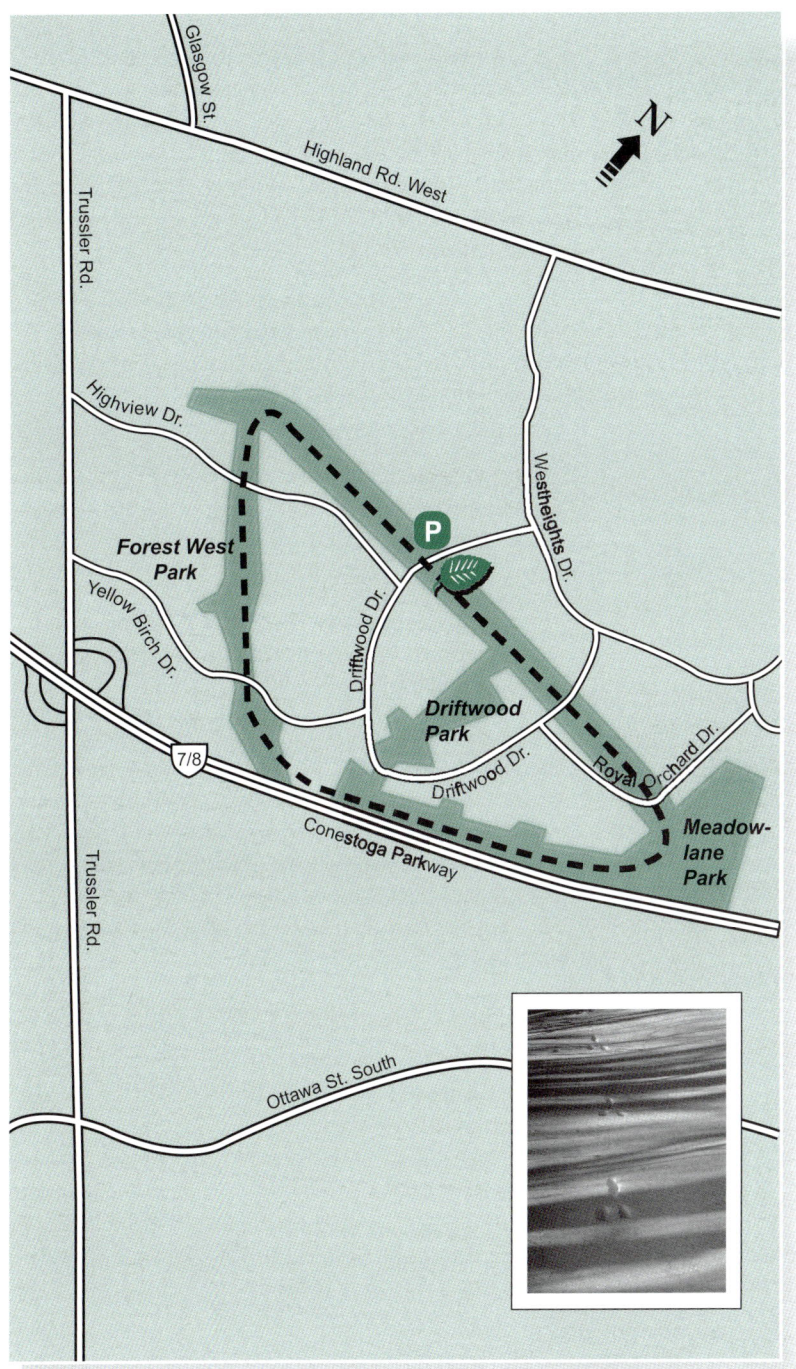

Elora Cataract Trailway, Belwood Lake to Orton

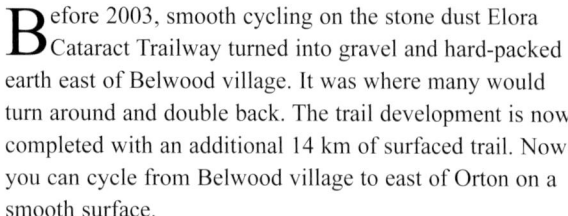

- 22 km linear

- Beginner

Before 2003, smooth cycling on the stone dust Elora Cataract Trailway turned into gravel and hard-packed earth east of Belwood village. It was where many would turn around and double back. The trail development is now completed with an additional 14 km of surfaced trail. Now you can cycle from Belwood village to east of Orton on a smooth surface.

Belwood Lake is a major starting point for this trail and in springtime, the drone of motors and water recreational vehicles don't accompany you on your journey. After leaving the water behind, the trail leads you past rolling hills, farmland and horses grazing in open fields.

The portion of the trail from Belwood Lake to Orton passes old stone houses, barns and open meadows. As the weather warms, wildflowers colour the trail, butterflies dart to and fro and a pale green highlights the forested areas.

Spring is also the time when this trail awakens with more users -- people riding horses, parents pushing baby carriages, teens walking their dogs.

Belwood Lake is a major starting point for this trail

Part of a 47 km rail-trail, this multi-use trailway links communities from Elora to Cataract. This former railway line also connects with the Trans Canada, Grand Valley and Bruce Trails. There are a few road crossings along this trail, so take caution if travelling with children. Remember to stay on the right when approaching oncoming users. And don't climb fences or take shortcuts -- most of the property bordering the trail is private.

TRAIL SURFACE: Stone dust, gravel.

IF YOU GO: From Highway 401 take Highway 6 North through Guelph to Fergus. From Highway 6 in Fergus, turn right/east on Belsyde Avenue (Wellington Road 18). You can park at Belwood Lake Conservation Area (phone 519-843-2979 - a modest admission fee applies for parking in season), or continue on and turn left onto Wellington Road 26 toward Belwood village, and park just after crossing the trail on Sideroad 10.

Elora Cataract Trailway, Belwood Lake to Orton

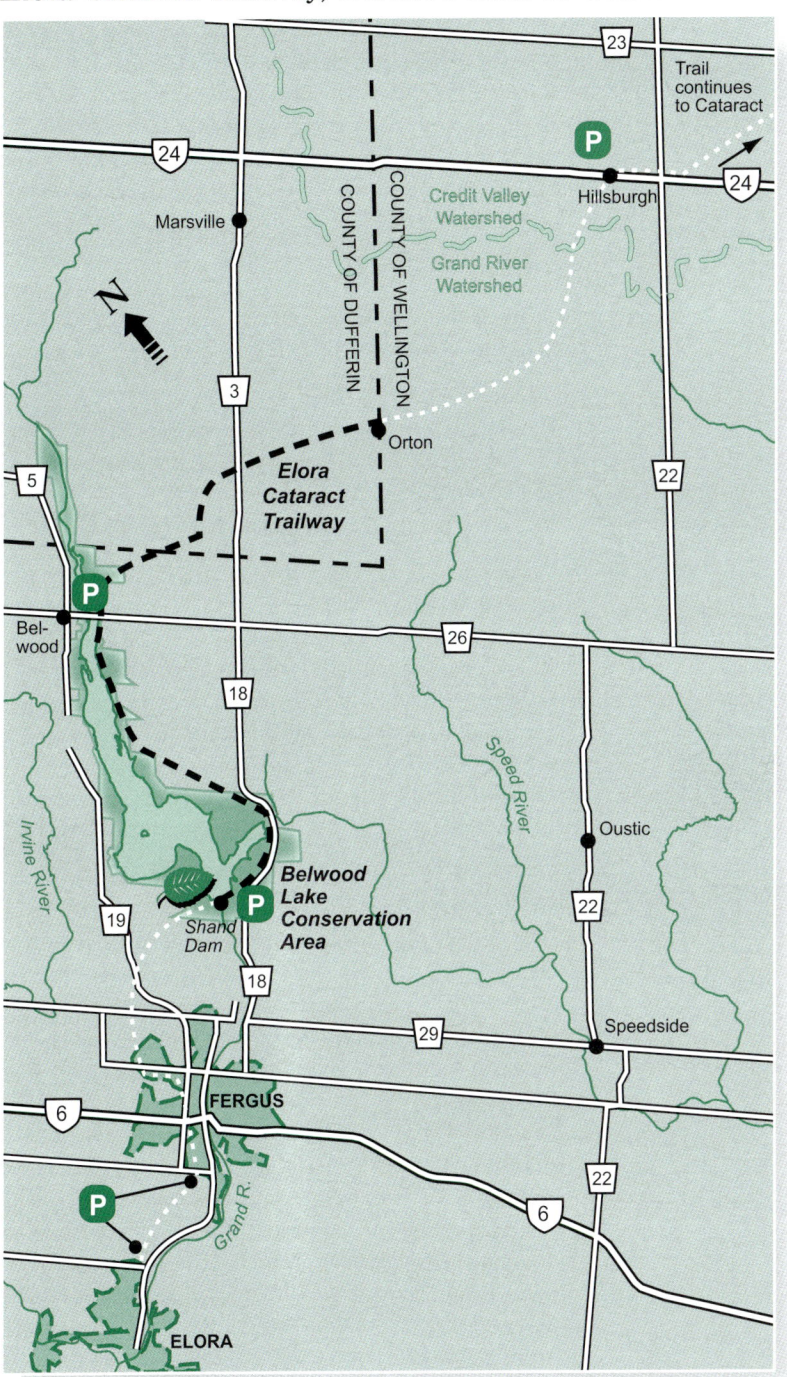

Foulds Trail, Cambridge

• **2.5 km linear**

• **Beginner**

There is magic in an oak forest. Often referred to as "mighty oaks," these trees were used by druids, bards and kings for important ceremonies and spiritual links to the land. Many old oaks were called "gospel oaks," relating to times when Druids met in mighty oak groves for meetings and teachings.

When you walk the Foulds Trail you'll be able to sit underneath an oak like an old Druid.

You'll hear the wind whisper through leaves, sounds that were interpreted as messages from the gods in the oracular oak grove at Dodona in Greece.

When you start out from the parking area, the trail dips through hills and valleys. Depending on the season, you'll round bends and find small pockets of water in the valley bottoms. Otherwise, when you reach the bend you'll find a larger wetland area.

Toward the end of the trail you'll leave the oaks behind and walk toward a red pine and Norway spruce plantation. This path seems to lead into a solid band of green, a straight path you walk into as if the trees are leading you forward. You'll have an open cornfield on your left side with large old trees bordering it as a natural fence line. This is an Agreement Forest, specifically planted as a tree plantation. The trail is an unmaintained access road, and although it is unmarked, the pathway is easy to follow.

There is magic
in an
oak forest

When you reach the road at the end of this trail you can return to the parking lot by walking along the concession, or you can follow the trail back. Take the trail. Sitting beneath an oak tree was believed to grant understanding, strength and spiritual renewal...perhaps the oaks will whisper you a message in the wind.

TRAIL SURFACE: Hard-packed earth.

IF YOU GO: From Highway 401 in Cambridge travel south on Highway 24. Take East River Road to Glen Morris. In Glen Morris, turn left on Princess Street (becomes McPherson School Road) and continue straight ahead, driving past Glen Morris Road. Continue onto the gravel road and cross over McLean School Road. You'll see the small parking area for Foulds on your right, soon after you cross the road.

Foulds Trail, Cambridge

Gordon Glaves - Waterworks Park Trail, Brantford

- 7.7 km linear

- Beginner

This paved trail starts at the top of a dike, originally built to hold back floodwaters. It now serves a dual function as part of the Gordon Glaves Memorial Pathway, a 40 km long trail, 26 of which also form part of the Trans Canada Trail, linking Hamilton and Cambridge.

The most interesting sections of this trail are the hard-packed earth and interpretive trails that branch off the main pathway and lead down into natural environments along the floodplain area. You'll notice many large cottonwood trees in this section as they can withstand both wet and dry conditions.

The paved trail is a flat section that winds along the river, opening up to views of the Grand at the south end as it winds and follows Grand River Avenue. At the north end of Waterworks Park (turning right when you reach the paved trail from the parking lot) you'll reach Wilkes Dam. In the 1800s, this weir used to channel water to feed downstream mills and the Grand River Canal. It now diverts water for Brantford's municipal water supply and is a popular fishing spot.

*The paved trail
winds along
the river*

If you continue south from Waterworks Park along the east side of the river, you'll be following the Trans Canada Trail. To follow the Glaves Memorial Pathway you need to cross the pedestrian bridge over the Grand below the Colborne Street bridge, and continue along the trail that follows the west side of the river along Gilkison Street, heading into Lion's Park. If you want a longer walk, this trail continues on to the Bell Homestead by following the white blazes of the Grand Valley Trail.

TRAIL SURFACE: Pavement.

IF YOU GO: From downtown Brantford, follow Brant Avenue and turn left on Scarfe Avenue. Drive down a steep hill and turn right on Grand River Avenue. Turn left on Woodland and park beside the Waterworks Park P.U.C. service depot.

Gordon Glaves - Waterworks Park Trail, Brantford

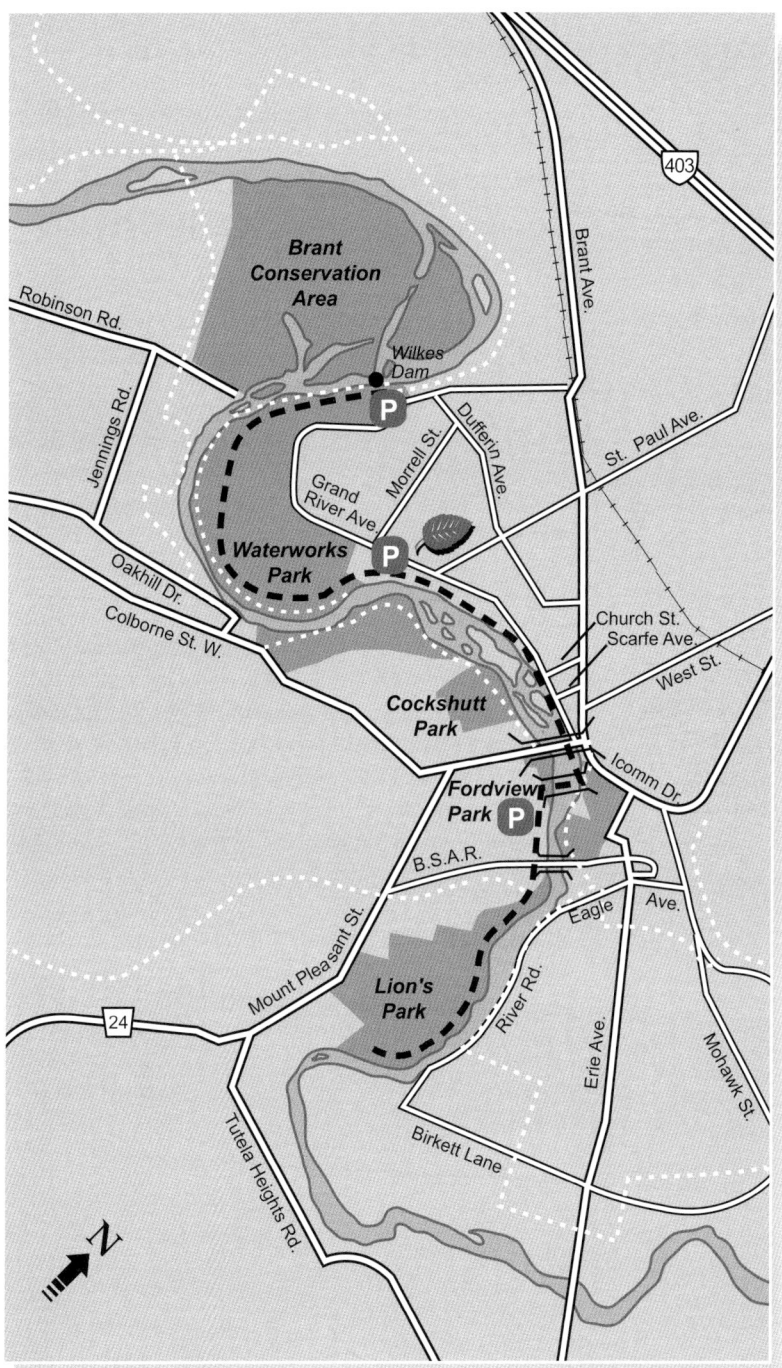

Jacob's Landing Trail, Cambridge

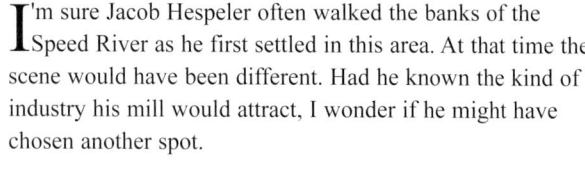

- 2 km linear
- Beginner

I'm sure Jacob Hespeler often walked the banks of the Speed River as he first settled in this area. At that time the scene would have been different. Had he known the kind of industry his mill would attract, I wonder if he might have chosen another spot.

If you start on this trail near the Mill Run Trail parking lot, you'll walk along Sheffield Street and turn right on Guelph Avenue before reaching a wooden lookout over the river by the dam across from American Standard. The walkway leading to this overlook is paved, passing through a park-like setting with benches.

It provides a scenic view of Old Hespeler over the millpond built by Jacob Hespeler, after whom the town was named. At the base of the dam, you'll see people fishing on sunny afternoons. Carp are the main catch.

You'll get a feel for what the river may have looked like in Jacob Hespeler's time, if you look further down the river that continues past the park. Although it looks like the trail continues on an earthen pathway along the banks of the Speed River, this is private property with no public trail easement. Although the paved trail ends at Jacob's Landing, make sure you take a side trail that leads to the water's edge where you may spot ducks, beaver and, if you look closely, see fish swimming near the banks.

People fishing on sunny afternoons

TRAIL SURFACE: Pavement, hard-packed earth.

IF YOU GO: From Highway 401, take the Highway 24 North exit and turn right on Queen Street into Hespeler. Turn left on Guelph Avenue and park on Milling Road or at the Sheffield Street parking lot.

Jacob's Landing Trail, Cambridge

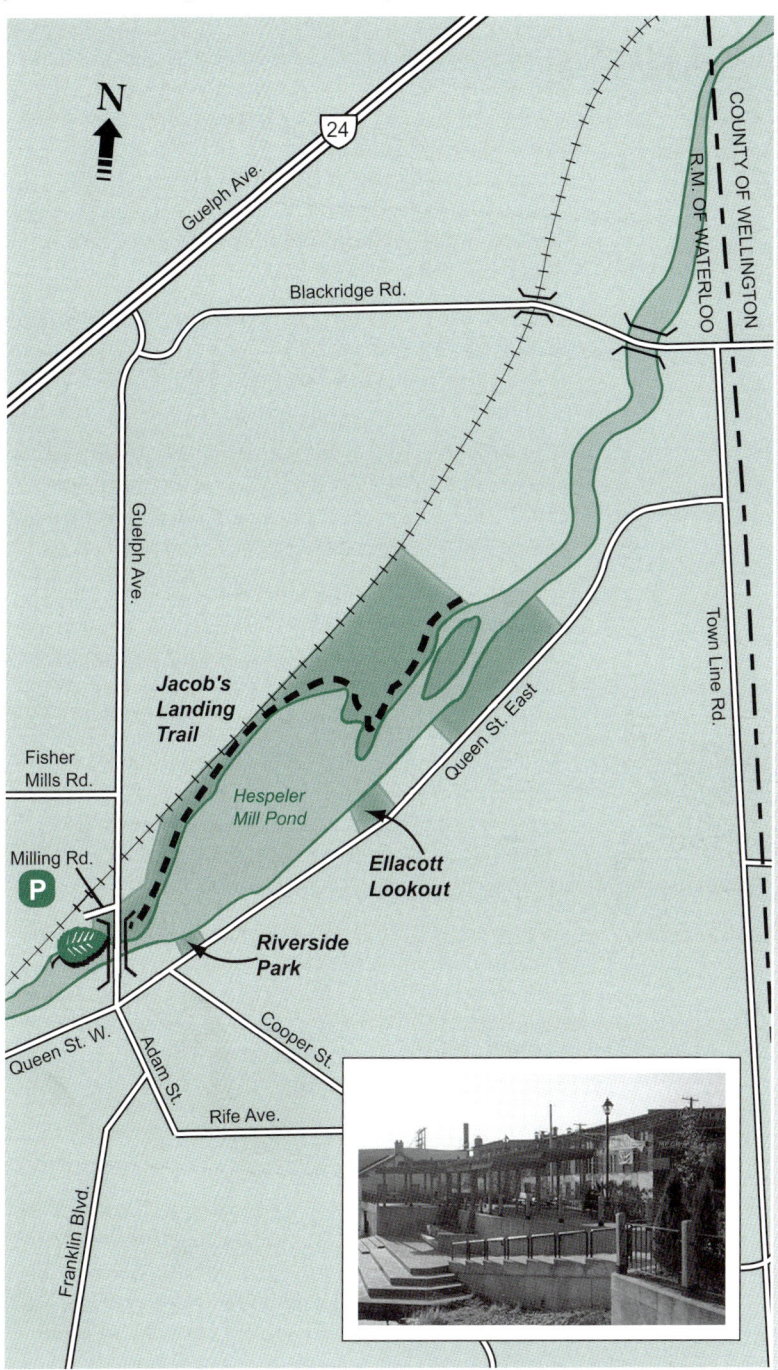

Kissing Bridge Trailway, Elmira

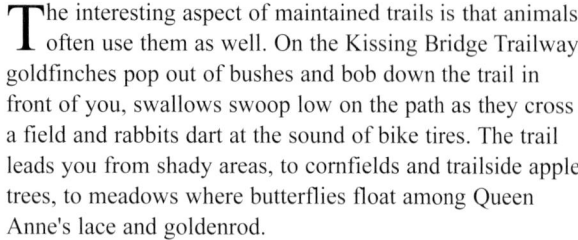

- 8 km linear trail (with 5.8 and 2 km linear trail options)

- Beginner

The interesting aspect of maintained trails is that animals often use them as well. On the Kissing Bridge Trailway, goldfinches pop out of bushes and bob down the trail in front of you, swallows swoop low on the path as they cross a field and rabbits dart at the sound of bike tires. The trail leads you from shady areas, to cornfields and trailside apple trees, to meadows where butterflies float among Queen Anne's lace and goldenrod.

These are some of the sights along this former Canadian Pacific Railway line that once ran from Guelph to Goderich. Part of the Trans Canada Trail, the section from Elmira to Wallenstein is complete with a wide stone dust surface.

After leaving the parking lot, head toward the Woolwich Observer building and cross the bridge over Canagagigue Creek. Make sure you look around and under the bridge as a mallard mother and her ducklings may be swimming nearby.

The trail continues past a park and memorial forest. This is a nice stop for children to run and stretch legs on the return trip. The trail crosses three bridges over Larches Creek and passes through countryside, cornfields, a horse pasture and a golf course.

This former Canadian Pacific Railway line once ran from Guelph to Goderich

For those who want a longer cycle on your return, you can continue over Regional Road 21 toward West Montrose. This is an extra 5.8 km linear portion of the trail. When you reach Regional Road 22 you also have a 2 km option to cycle to the West Montrose Kissing Bridge.

After Regional Road 22, the wide stone dust trail ends and it becomes a one-lane hard-packed earth track. There is a meadow with some picnic tables, but the trail eventually dead-ends at a danger sign. There is a deep chasm over a creek where there used to be a bridge. Don't take the road to the left because it's a private road that leads to a farmer's field.

TRAIL SURFACE: Stone dust (hard-packed earth on a 2.9 km portion).

IF YOU GO: From Conestoga Parkway in Waterloo, continue toward Elmira. The road becomes Regional Road 21 and then Arthur Street South. After crossing Riverside Drive, look for the Kissing Bridge Trailway sign on your left, before the Woolwich Observer building. If the parking lot is full, street parking is also available.

Kissing Bridge Trailway, Elmira

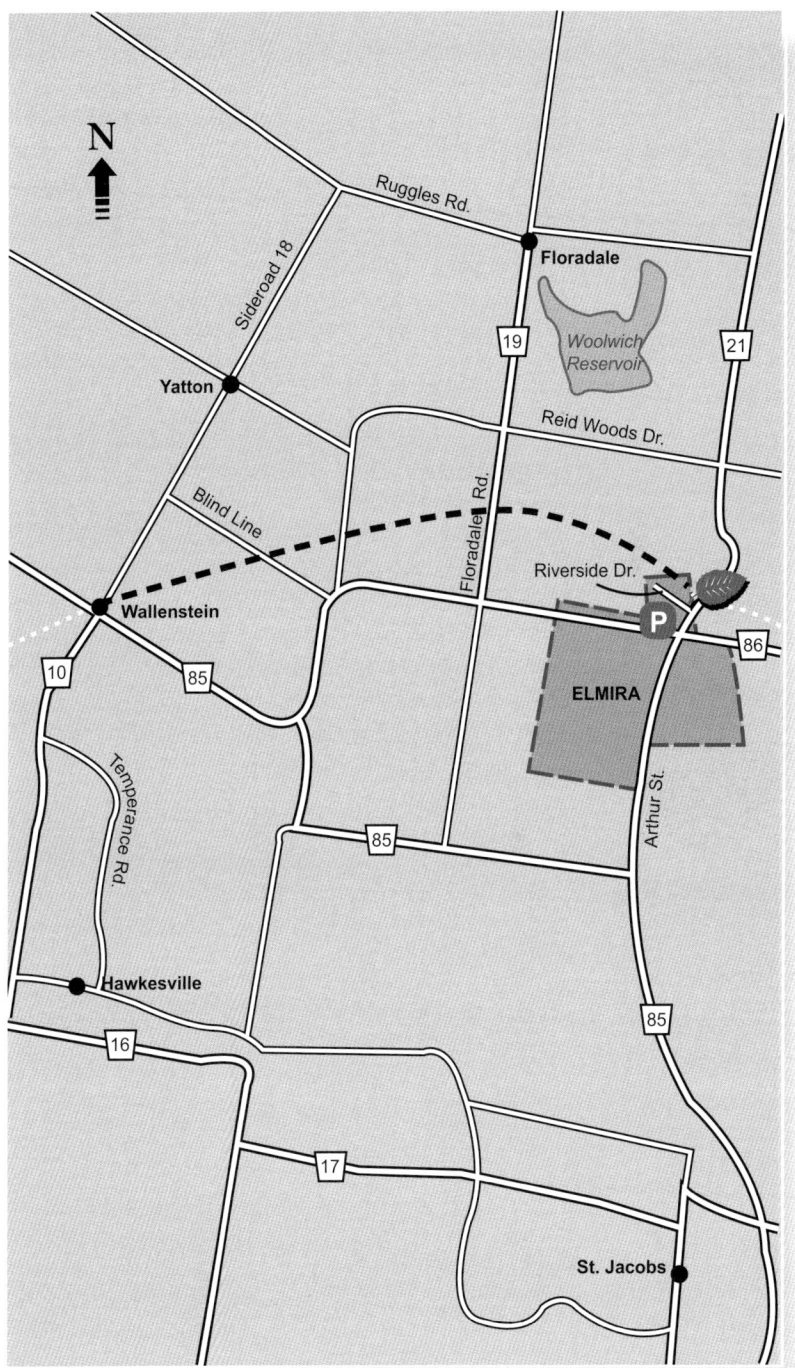

Lakeside Park Trail, Kitchener

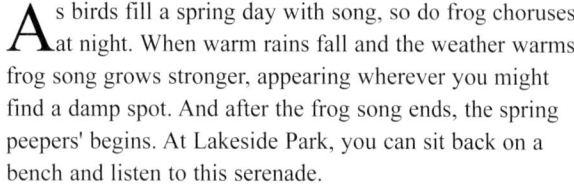

- 2.5 km linear

- Beginner

As birds fill a spring day with song, so do frog choruses at night. When warm rains fall and the weather warms, frog song grows stronger, appearing wherever you might find a damp spot. And after the frog song ends, the spring peepers' begins. At Lakeside Park, you can sit back on a bench and listen to this serenade.

Although this trail follows Westmount Road for a while and then goes under the Conestoga Parkway, it eventually leads into Concordia Park, ending at Lakeside. The only other diversion is a walk behind the Greenbrook water treatment plant to continue the Lakeside Park Trail from its parking lot.

You might hear frogs chorus during the day, but it's mostly at night that the lake will burst with sound. If you enjoy listening for frogs, you might want to join Amphibian Call Counts, a survey program that estimates the abundance of frogs and toads based on their distinctive calls. "Road Call Counts" cover designated routes by car on three evenings each spring, during which frogs and toads are surveyed at 10 three-minute stops placed every 0.8 km. Backyard surveys take place in or near backyards for three minutes every night from April to August. For more information, call the Canadian Wildlife Federation at 1-800-563-WILD

When warm rains fall and the weather warms, frog song grows stronger

TRAIL SURFACE: Hard-packed earth and grass.

IF YOU GO: From the Conestoga Parkway, take the Homer Watson Boulevard North exit. Turn left onto Stirling and right on Greenbrook Drive. Turn right on Lakeside Drive and park along the road.

Lakeside Park Trail, Kitchener

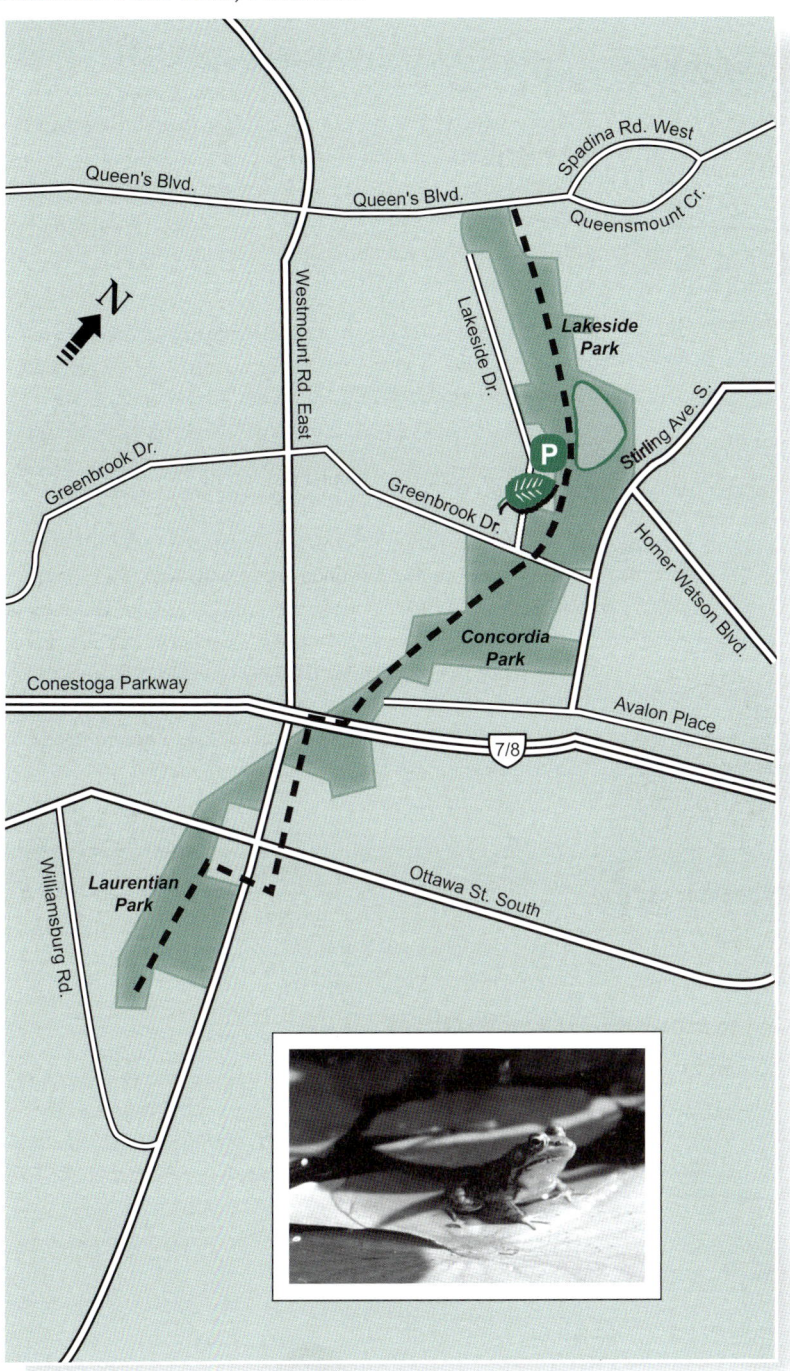

Linear Trail, Cambridge

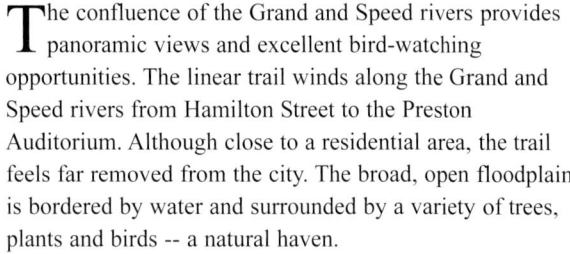

- 2.5 km linear
- Beginner

The confluence of the Grand and Speed rivers provides panoramic views and excellent bird-watching opportunities. The linear trail winds along the Grand and Speed rivers from Hamilton Street to the Preston Auditorium. Although close to a residential area, the trail feels far removed from the city. The broad, open floodplain is bordered by water and surrounded by a variety of trees, plants and birds -- a natural haven.

More than 150 species of birds have been spotted along this trail. Mallards, Canada geese and green herons are plentiful, but you'll also see Baltimore orioles, European starlings, warbling vireos and red-eyed vireos. Bring along binoculars to spot house finches, goldfinches and cedar waxwings. You'll need a birding field guide to identify cliff swallows, bank swallows and tree swallows.

The confluence of the Grand River and Speed River provides excellent bird watching opportunities

This natural trail is also an historical one. An industrial site since the early 19th century, the area now occupied by apartments and townhouses was once a tannery and later the site of the Bernhardt Rock Brewery. The hill near Cruickston Park was the site of a log cabin in 1790. Today, it's surrounded by houses. At the end of the trail you'll see a gristmill built in 1807, one of the oldest continuously operating industrial sites in the Region of Waterloo.

You'll also see dolomitic limestone cliffs that were formed about 450 million years ago. These outcrops are the result of reefs created when this entire area was part of the Michigan Basin, a tropical sea. These Silurian marine rocks contain marine invertebrate fossils.

TRAIL SURFACE: Stone dust.

IF YOU GO: From Highway 401 and Kitchener, take Highway 8 south toward Cambridge. At the bottom of the hill on Shantz Hill Road, turn left onto Fountain Street and at the first set of lights, turn right on King Street. Turn right on Eagle Street, left on Hamilton Street and park in the Preston Auditorium parking lot on the corner of Bishop Street and Hamilton Street.

Linear Trail, Cambridge

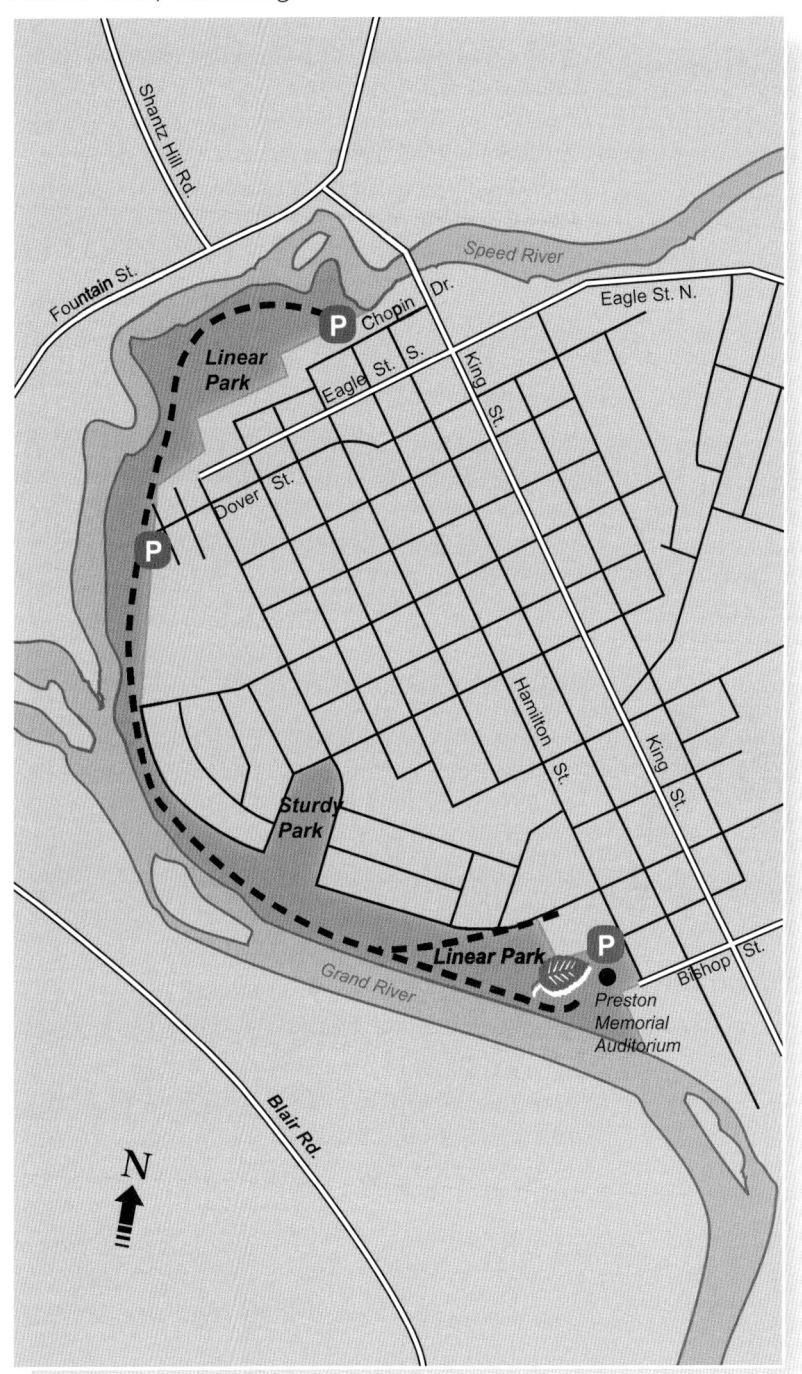

Little Tract Trail, Cambridge

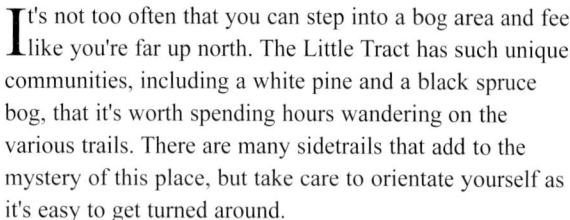

- 3.7 km linear

- Beginner

It's not too often that you can step into a bog area and feel like you're far up north. The Little Tract has such unique communities, including a white pine and a black spruce bog, that it's worth spending hours wandering on the various trails. There are many sidetrails that add to the mystery of this place, but take care to orientate yourself as it's easy to get turned around.

The Little Tract dates back to 1839 when the 200 acres were settled by Robert Little. In 1946, John Little donated the 200 acres to the County of Wellington. This land is now designated a provincially significant wetland area.

The trail winds up and down little hills left behind by the Wisconsin glacial period. The boulders, which can be seen in the old stone fence rows, combined with steep hills, made this land difficult to farm. About two-thirds of the Little Tract was once an agricultural desert.

The upland woods of sugar maple, beech and hemlock have been disturbed through forestry practices, but toward the north end, about one-third is still old growth remnant.

Upland woods of sugar maple, beech and hemlock

The trail passes through a variety of terrains, from swamp-bog community and lowland swamp forest to upland deciduous forest and pine plantations. Wherever you turn, you feel like you're walking deeper and deeper into a dense forest.

Make sure you listen for the slow, musical trill of the swamp sparrow. It's difficult to spot this shy bird as it spends much of its time in impassable sections of the bog.

TRAIL SURFACE: Gravel, hard-packed earth with rocks and grass. (Some areas near the water can be muddy.)

IF YOU GO: From Highway 401 east of Cambridge, take the Highway 6 North exit. Turn left on County Road 34 and after passing through Aikensville and crossing Sideroad 10 North, look for the Little Tract parking lot on your right.

Little Tract Trail, Cambridge

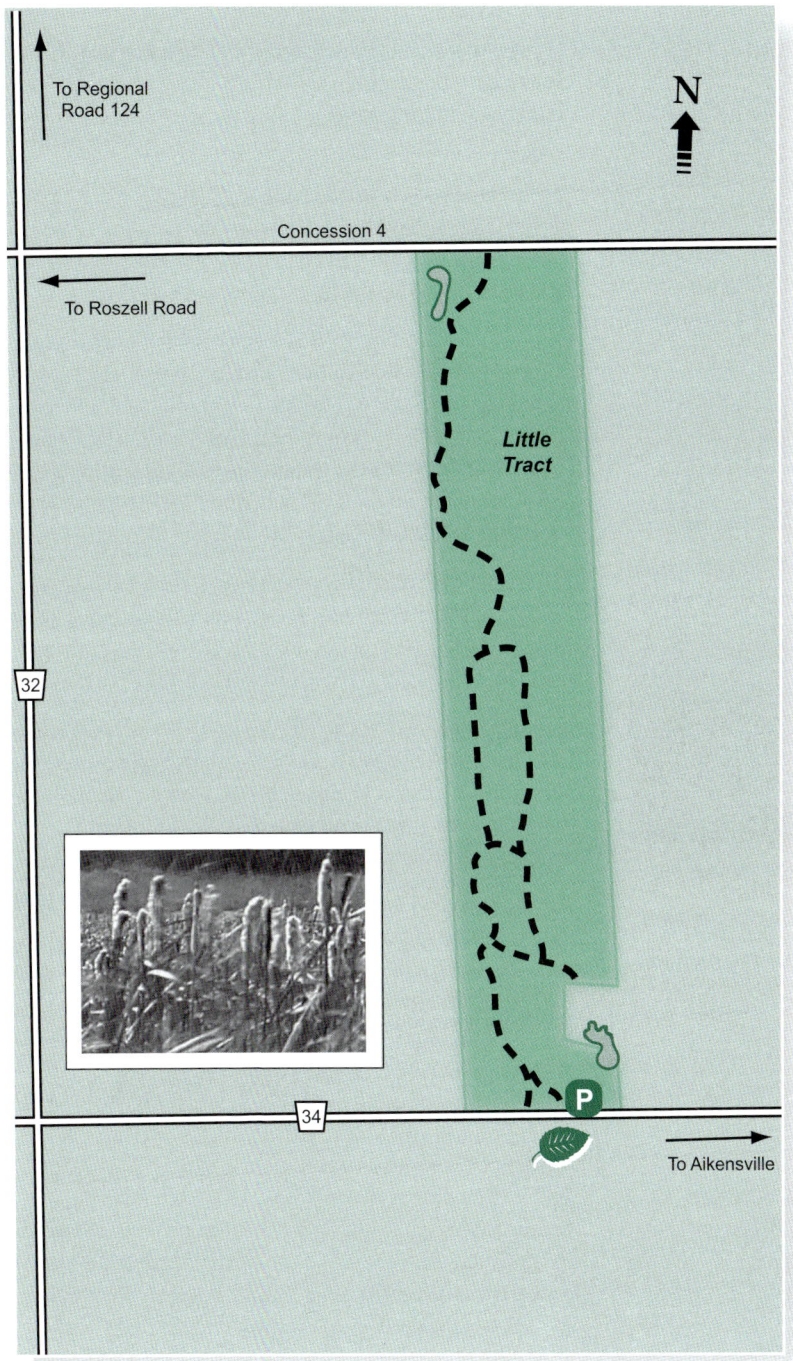

To Regional Road 124

N

Concession 4

To Roszell Road

Little Tract

32

34

P

To Aikensville

Maryhill Cycling Trail, Bloomingdale

- 23 km loop
- Beginner

Ease into cycling with a longer trail that has gentle grades. This country cycle has a unique European setting and interesting stops along the way with everything from golf balls to antiques for sale.

The beginning stretch along Crowsfoot Road is quite flat and good to build up speed and warm up your muscles. Although a country road, at some times of the year you can find large farm machines so be careful if cycling with children.

Before you cross Maryhill Road, you'll pass through a variety of scenery on this section, from a pottery shop to open countryside and thick woodlands. If you want a shorter loop, and to avoid Sawmill Road, which is a busier roadway, you can turn right onto Beitz. (Durant is another option but it's gravel.) If you want a longer route, you can detour onto Pine Creek Road from St. Charles.

Turn right on St. Charles Street and cycle the winding road through gentle hills and open woodland. There are stops along the way, from antique shops to a pick-your-own-strawberry farm.

As you round one of the bends, you reach the highlight of this trail. Maryhill sits in the distance, the church spire reaching toward the sky from the hilltop. It's the closest you'll get to a European setting, where hilltop towns are perched in the middle of the countryside.

As you come into town, turn right on Maryhill Road to see the church and the old cemetery behind it. The rest of the cycling route takes you past wide, open fields that stretch as far as the eye can see. When you pedal into Bloomingdale, turn right on Sawmill Road and cycle for two kilometres back to Crowsfoot Road.

TRAIL SURFACE: Pavement.

IF YOU GO: From Kitchener, take Highway 7 toward Guelph. Turn left on Sawmill Road (Regional Road 17). Pass Waterloo Regional Road 52 and continue on Sawmill Road and drive through Bloomingdale. When you reach the turnoff for Katherine Street (Regional Road 23), take a sharp right onto Crowsfoot Road and park along the side of the road.

The church spire reaches toward the sky from the hilltop

Maryhill Cycling Trail, Bloomingdale

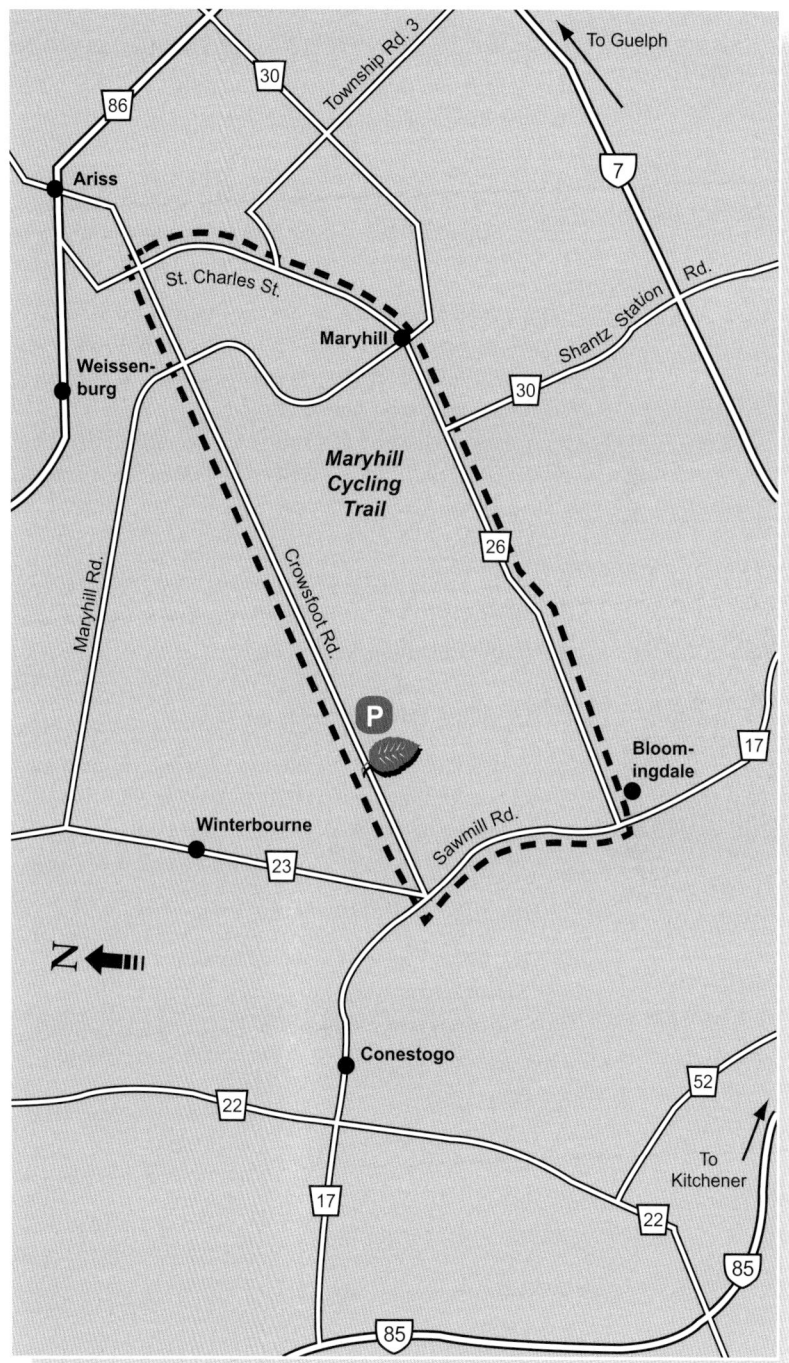

Mill Race Trail, St. Jacobs

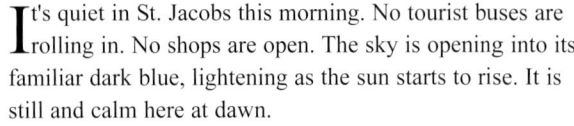

- 2 km linear
- Beginner

It's quiet in St. Jacobs this morning. No tourist buses are rolling in. No shops are open. The sky is opening into its familiar dark blue, lightening as the sun starts to rise. It is still and calm here at dawn.

The Mill Race trail is one of the lesser-known trails in St. Jacobs. A hidden walkway where locals can duck away from the hustle and bustle that often descends on this small town.

From the red caboose, cross over the footbridge and walk toward the waterway. The trail is lined by the millrace on the left and, behind the trees, the Conestogo River on the right. There are scenic spots to catch a moment of repose -- benches along the trail and a cement structure to lean against near the river. In 1897 willow trees were planted along the millrace to offer shade for villagers strolling on a hot summer day.

The trail leads to the Conestogo River, the feeder for the waterway you have been walking along. The millrace is a man-made waterway where water was diverted from the dam to the mill pond. Built in the 1860s, the millrace contributed to the development of St. Jacobs as it was used to power the mill. You're walking along history on this trail.

You're also walking into the morning. The sounds greet you. Birds chirp their morning song. A dog barks in the distance. A horse clops along the street pulling a horse-drawn buggy. Extend this trail and venture into town...it's still waking up.

Willow trees offer shade for villagers strolling on a hot summer day

TRAIL SURFACE: Hard-packed earth, gravel, stone dust.

IF YOU GO: Take the Conestoga Parkway (Highway 85) North from Waterloo and follow signs that lead to St. Jacobs. From King Street in downtown St. Jacobs, turn onto Front Street, pass the silo shops and park near the red caboose.

Mill Race Trail, St. Jacobs

Mill Run Trail, Cambridge

- 7.5 km linear

- Beginner

They start early in the morning, waking up the sun with a blend of high-pitched melodies, whistling crescendos, trills and chirps. On many woodland trails you'll find a variety of birds, each with a distinct song. Together they harmonize, their faithful renditions filling woodlands with a sure sign of spring.

The Mill Run Trail offers a great opportunity for spotting birds. The trail follows the former Galt, Preston, Hespeler Electric Railway line, hugging the Speed River, passing by bulrushes in wetland areas and cutting through wooded areas such as Chilligo Conservation Area. In some sections the trees are so thick that they form a canopy over the trail. This is one of the most scenic trails in Cambridge with many bridge crossings and wide river vistas.

If you walk early in the morning, the Mill Run is alive with birds and their song. You may also spot deer feeding near the river's edge, beaver ambling along the banks or ducks swimming through the mist as it rises from the river.

When you reach Beaverdale Road, turn left and walk across the bridge. The trail continues on the opposite side of the road, eventually crossing underneath Highway 401 and continuing onto Speedsville Street and into Riverside Park.

Look for marsh marigold, mayapples, trout lillies, Canada violet and trilliums

Make sure you take this trail in the spring when wildflowers are abundant. Look for marsh marigold, mayapples, trout lilies, Canada violet and trilliums.

TRAIL SURFACE: Stone dust, hard-packed earth, boardwalk and bridges.

IF YOU GO: From Highway 401, take the Hespeler Road (Highway 24) North exit and then turn right on Queen Street into Hespeler. Turn left on Guelph Avenue, and left on Sheffield Street. You'll see the trailhead sign and parking lot on your left.

Mill Run Trail, Cambridge

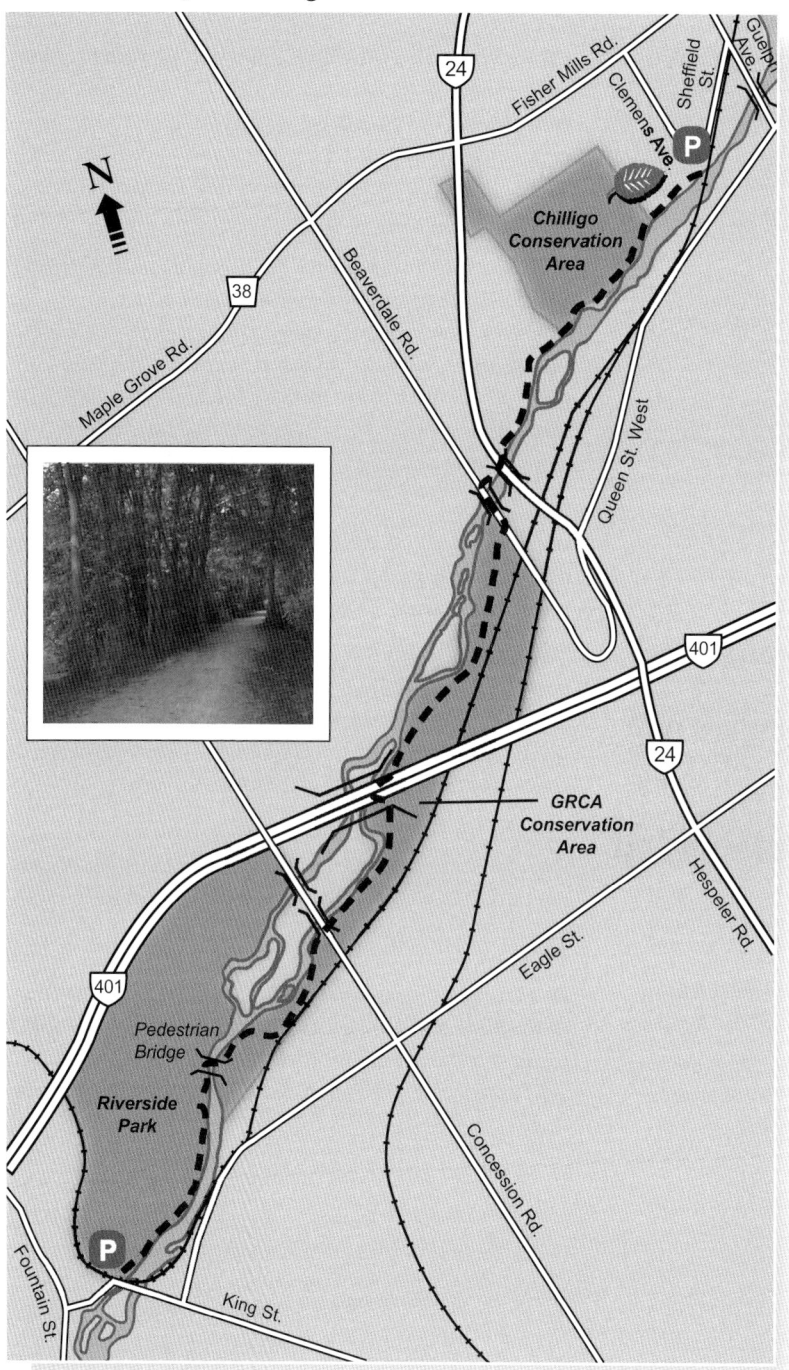

RIM Park Trail, Waterloo

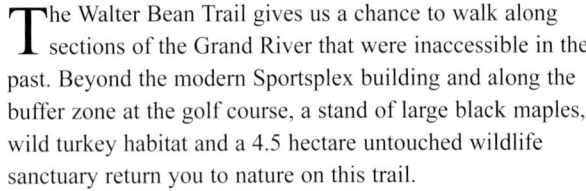

- 4 km linear
- Beginner

The Walter Bean Trail gives us a chance to walk along sections of the Grand River that were inaccessible in the past. Beyond the modern Sportsplex building and along the buffer zone at the golf course, a stand of large black maples, wild turkey habitat and a 4.5 hectare untouched wildlife sanctuary return you to nature on this trail.

The wetland section along the Walter Bean Trail that runs through RIM Park is an important wildlife corridor for amphibians and reptiles. Walk gently through this area, a delicate piece of habitat, protected by culverts that offer passage to these creatures from the wetland to the nature sanctuary.

It's one of many unique environmental aspects of this trail. The creek you pass has been rehabilitated. Around the oxbow, you'll see a grove of bitternut hickory, a Carolinian species out of its normal range. In this section, a line of willows also marks the old bank of the river.

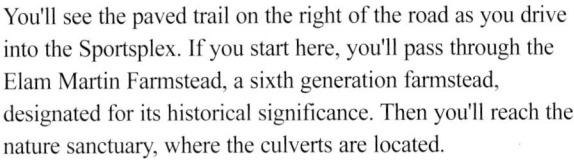

You'll see the paved trail on the right of the road as you drive into the Sportsplex. If you start here, you'll pass through the Elam Martin Farmstead, a sixth generation farmstead, designated for its historical significance. Then you'll reach the nature sanctuary, where the culverts are located.

There are two small sections on this trail where you'll share the space with golf carts, but this minimizes the impact of the road since those areas are main corridors for wildlife.

An 11-acre untouched nature sanctuary

TRAIL SURFACE: Pavement.

IF YOU GO: From Conestoga Parkway take the University Avenue East exit. You'll see the Sportsplex on your right. You can park at the Sportsplex or near the wooden Walter Bean Trail kiosk before the Park House at Grey Silo Golf Course.

RIM Park Trail, Waterloo

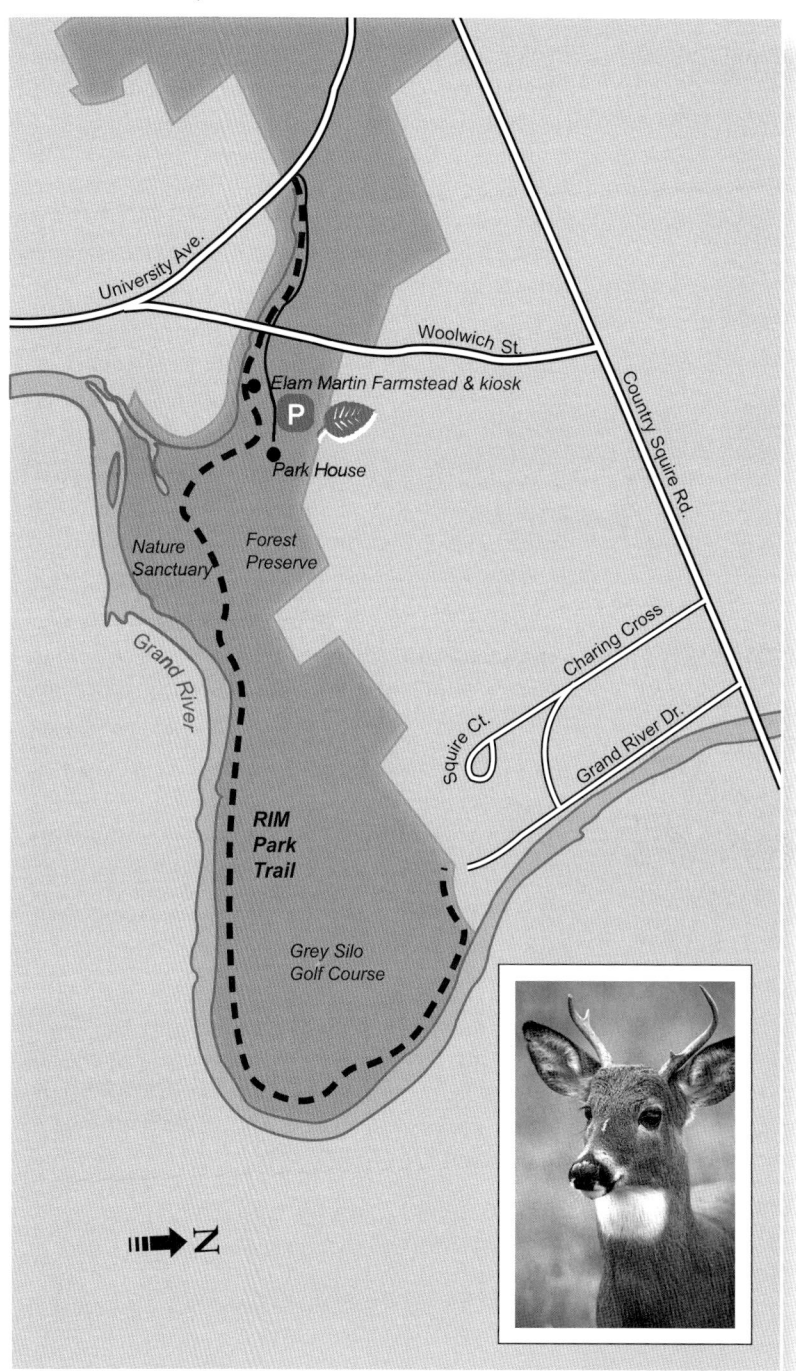

University Ave.

Woolwich St.

Country Squire Rd.

Elam Martin Farmstead & kiosk

P

Park House

Nature Sanctuary

Forest Preserve

Grand River

Charing Cross

Squire Ct.

Grand River Dr.

RIM Park Trail

Grey Silo Golf Course

N

Riverside Park Loop, Cambridge

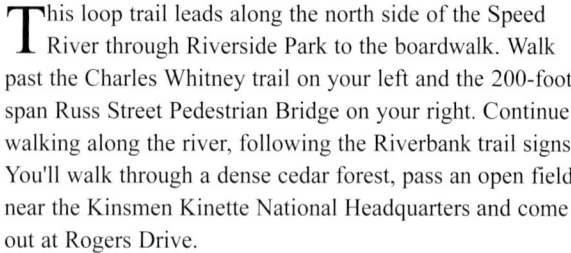

- 4 km loop
- Beginner

This loop trail leads along the north side of the Speed River through Riverside Park to the boardwalk. Walk past the Charles Whitney trail on your left and the 200-foot span Russ Street Pedestrian Bridge on your right. Continue walking along the river, following the Riverbank trail signs. You'll walk through a dense cedar forest, pass an open field near the Kinsmen Kinette National Headquarters and come out at Rogers Drive.

Turn right on Speedsville Road, cross over the bridge and on your right hand side, follow the sign for the Mill Run trail. This return loop is on the newest portion of the 7.5 km Mill Run trail.

As you walk along the Speed River, especially through Riverside Park, you'll see ducks swimming in the river and waddling onto the banks.

You might want to bring some seeds for the chickadees on the Charles Whitney Boardwalk trail. It's located on your right as you leave the boardwalk area. This is one of the friendliest chickadee areas. If you hold still, they'll eat seeds right from your hand.

Chickadees eat seeds right from your hands

Be careful when walking this and all trails in the winter as there are icy patches that can be very slippery. Make sure you walk slowly over them or take a walking stick to help with balance.

TRAIL SURFACE: Pavement, boardwalk, hard-packed earth.

IF YOU GO: From Kitchener, take Highway 8 toward Cambridge. At the bottom of the hill on Shantz Hill Road, turn left onto Fountain Street and right on King Street at the first set of lights. As you round the bend you'll see Riverside Park on your left. There are parking lots both inside and outside the main gates.

Riverside Park Loop, Cambridge

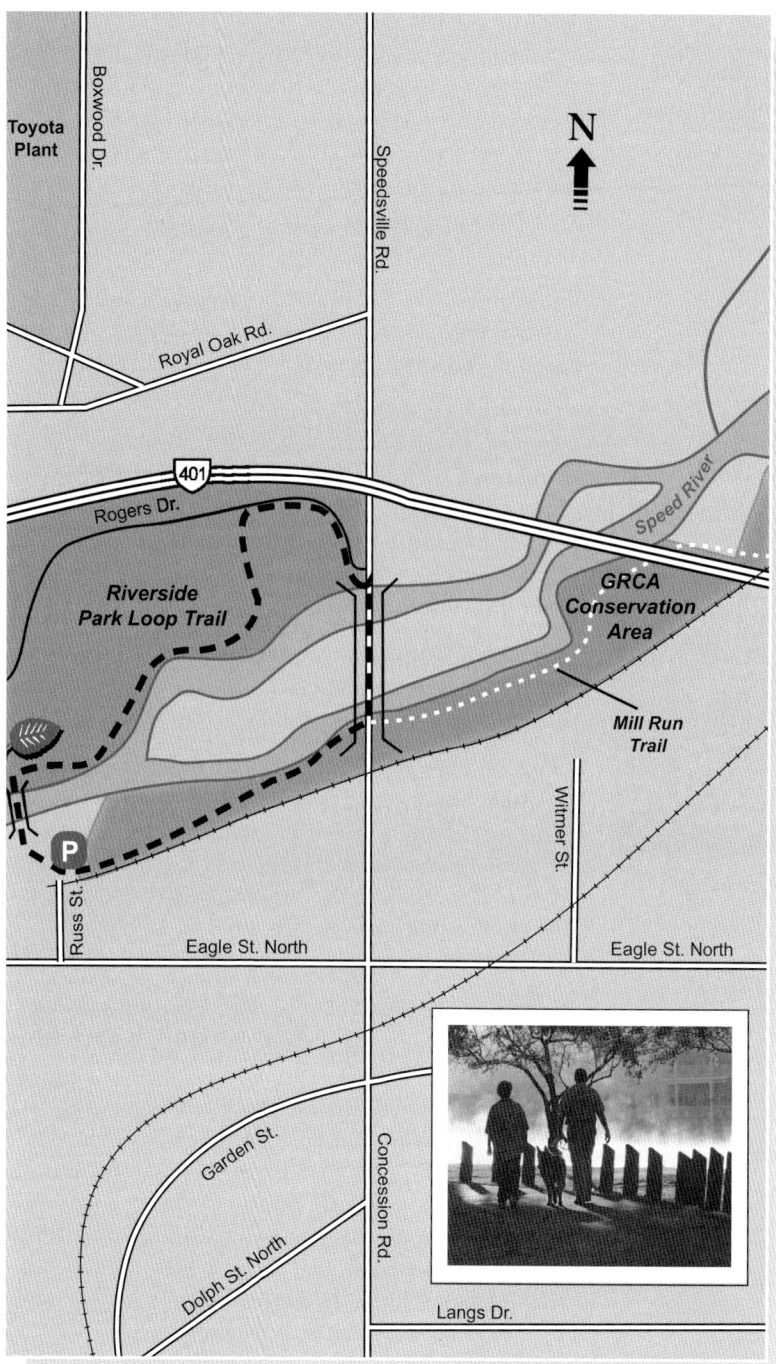

Toyota Plant

Boxwood Dr.

Royal Oak Rd.

Speedsville Rd.

N

401

Rogers Dr.

Speed River

Riverside Park Loop Trail

GRCA Conservation Area

Mill Run Trail

Witmer St.

P

Russ St.

Eagle St. North

Eagle St. North

Garden St.

Concession Rd.

Dolph St. North

Langs Dr.

Rockway Gardens Trail, Kitchener

- 1.5 km loop
- Beginner

Since I was a little girl holding on to my grandpa's hand, I have wandered through Rockway Gardens, stepping onto rocks as if they were mountains and imagining the crevasses as giant caves. Perhaps others who have walked through, driven past or visited the gardens during a wedding, have found another perspective beyond the tulips, fountains and 50,000 annuals.

Rockway Gardens, built in 1933, was designed to highlight the physical features across Canada from east to west coast. The original plans were destroyed in a fire in the 1950s, so we must use our imagination when walking through the gardens.

The cascade and fishpond on the south side represent the five Great Lakes. The second pond, with three cascades, portrays Lake Winnipeg, Great Bear Lake and Great Slave Lake on the edge of the Canadian Shield. Scattered rocks among the central fountain on the north side depict the Arctic Ocean, James Bay and Hudson Bay.

Annual beds with more than 53 varieties

There isn't a distinct pathway that leads through the gardens, but you can meander from one garden plot to another, pause at one of the ponds and walk up the stairway to the upper level.

When you walk up these stairs to the top area of the golf course, you are entering the higher, steeper areas of Canada's West coast. The scattered rocks to the right of the staircase represent the outer islands on the west coast. Similarly, an isolated flowerbed near the garden house on the east side depicts the Atlantic provinces.

These interpretations are left to the imagination, so wander the gardens and come up with your own! Also pause at the various flowerbeds: 300-by-20 foot perennial border, annual beds with more than 53 varieties and a native wildflower garden filled with birds, butterflies and bees. Make sure to visit again in mid-July as the flowerbeds fill in and the blooms spread.

TRAIL SURFACE: Grass, pavement.

IF YOU GO: From Highway 401, take the Highway 8 exit to Kitchener. After passing under the Conestoga Parkway, turn left onto Preston Street and then left onto Floral Crescent. You may park along this street and walk the grounds.

Rockway Gardens Trail, Kitchener

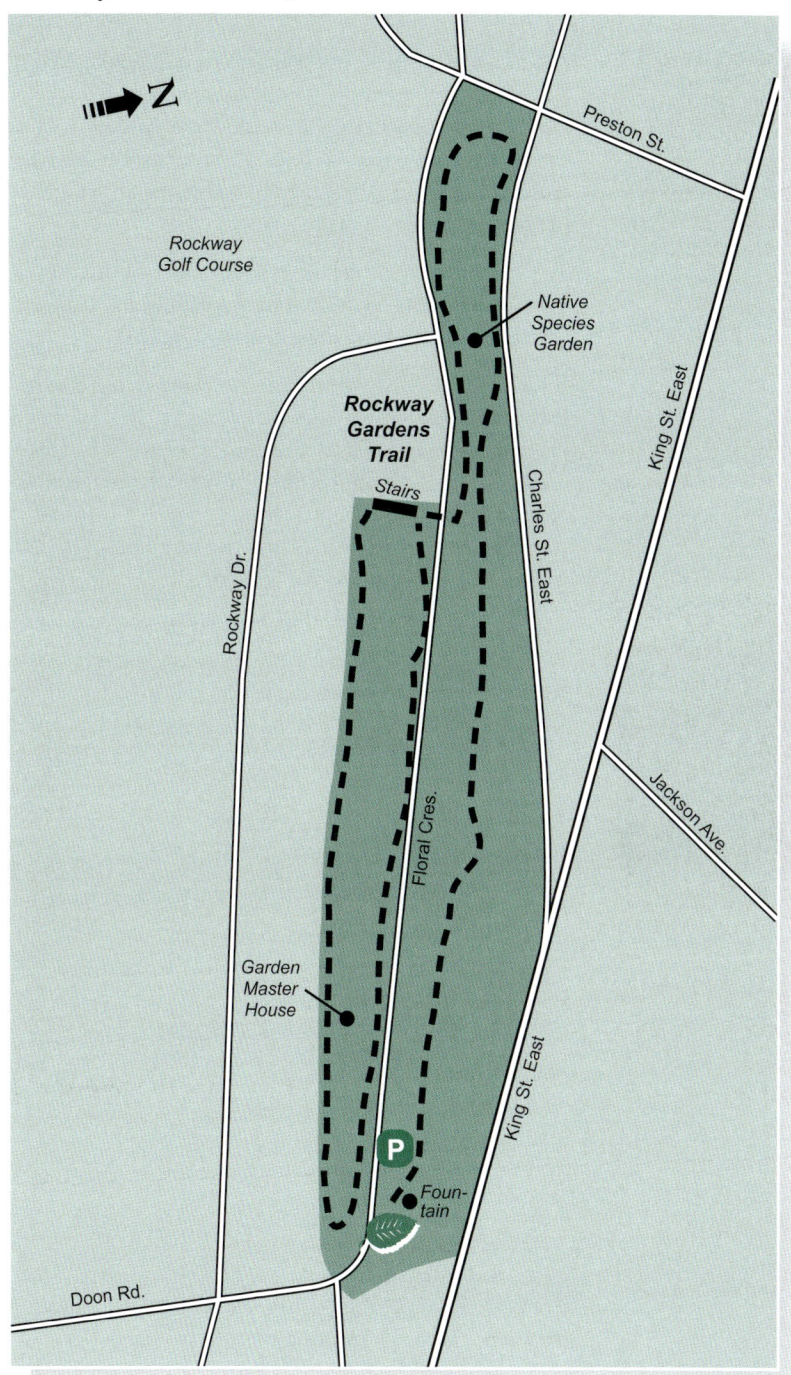

Rockwood - Gilbert MacIntyre Trail, Rockwood

• 3.5 km linear
(other area
trails: partial
loops)

• Beginner to
Intermediate

The Eramosa River meets limestone cliffs, caves and glacial potholes as it ambles its way through Rockwood. About 23,000 years ago, the retreat of the Wisconsin glacier carved Rockwood Conservation Area's landscape, leaving more than 200 glacial potholes measuring up to six metres (20 feet) wide and 12 metres (40 feet) deep.

The trail starts behind the beach house with a steep, rocky climb, then heads into the forest and passes by the water's edge, a small cave and a large rock outcrop.

A large group of glacial potholes is located near the boardwalk area. Others can be seen from the lookout on the other side of the water. The glacial meltwaters swirled small rocks, large granite stones and sand with such force that they cut into the rock, creating these cylindrical holes.

From the boardwalk that now forms part of the Gilbert MacIntyre Memorial Trail, you'll pass ruins of an old woolen and grist mill, run by the Harris family from 1867 to 1925. Within the interior of the ruin is a bridge crossing over a small brook that leads to a picnic area.

The rest of the trail leads through a forested area with one lookout that offers a grand view of the park.

TRAIL SURFACE: Hard-packed earth with rocks, tree roots and grass.

IF YOU GO: From Highway 401, take Exit 312, Guelph Line. Travel north on Guelph Line and turn right onto Highway 7. Continue until you see signs for Rockwood Conservation Area on your right. The park phone number is (519) 856-9543 and an admission fee applies in season.

The Eramosa River meets limestone cliffs, caves and glacial potholes

Rockwood - Gilbert MacIntyre Trail, Rockwood

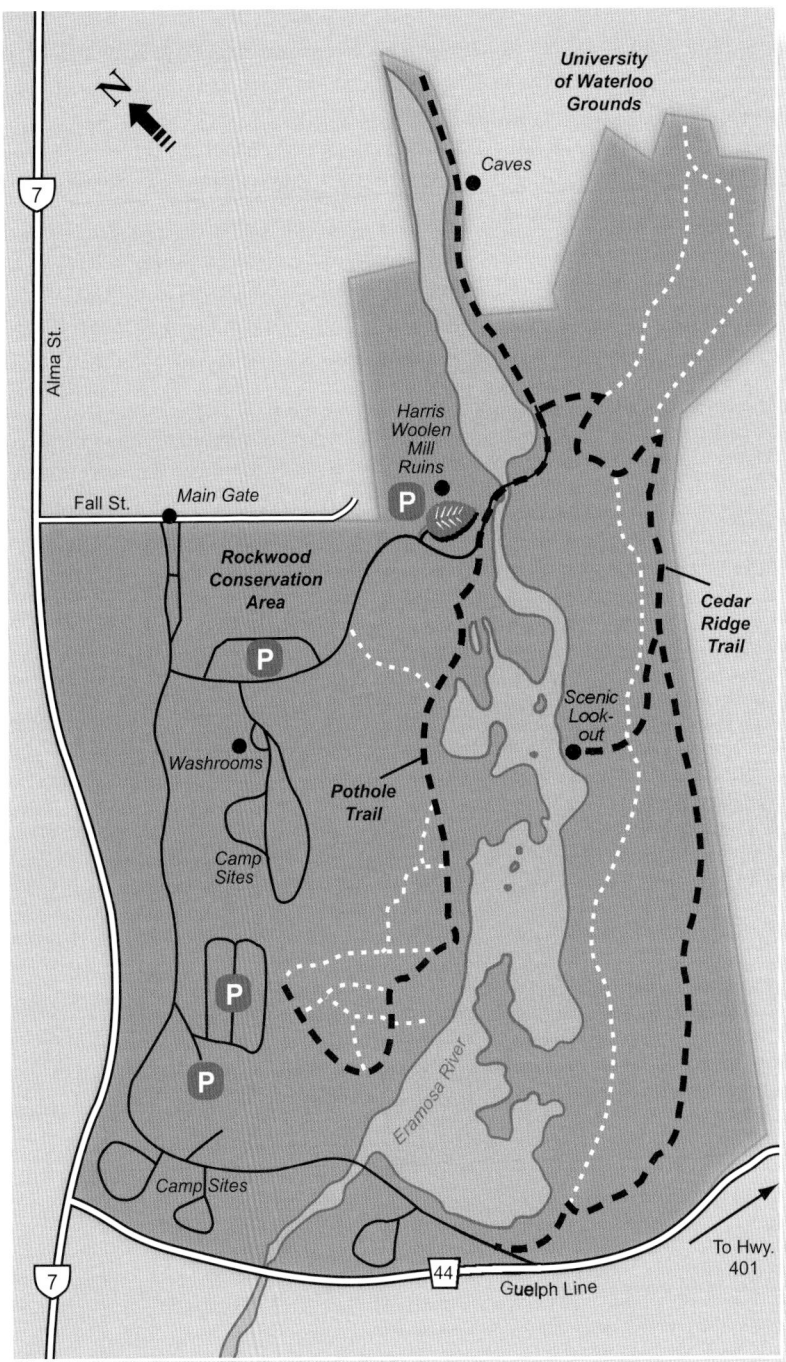

Royal Recreation Downtown Trail, Guelph

- 3.6 km linear

- Beginner

A tablet marks the spot where John Galt, general agent of the Canada Company, cut the first tree in founding the City of Guelph on April 23, 1827. You'll face it when crossing Macdonell and Wellington streets. From here, the trail slopes down toward a narrow part of the river into Heritage Park.

In 1830, a wooden mill was erected on this site by Horace Perry for the Canada Company. Now in its place stands a cairn, built from ruins of a five-storey stone mill constructed by William Allan of Killochan, Ayrshire, Scotland.

From the ruins, the trail continues along the Speed River where trees line the banks, and icicles hang from rooftops of old stone buildings in the winter. When you reach Wyndham Street, walk across the bridge to the other side of the river and continue on the trail from there. You'll pass behind an industrial area and then head toward a covered bridge. This area marks the confluence of the Speed and Eramosa rivers. It's also a connector to the 4.1 km Eramosa River Trail.

As you walk along this trail, you're bound to see ducks in the river's open channels. If you continue over the covered bridge, you can continue along the other side of the Speed River by crossing Gordon Street. When you reach the McCrae Street stone bridge, you can cross to the other side of the river and explore the open fields in the park.

You're bound to see ducks in the river's open channels

TRAIL SURFACE: Hard-packed earth, gravel, stone dust, paved.

IF YOU GO: From Highway 401 go north on Guelph's Hanlon Expressway/Highway 6 and turn right on Wellington Street. After the railway overpass, turn left on Macdonell Street and park in the metered parking area on your right.

Royal Recreation Downtown Trail, Guelph

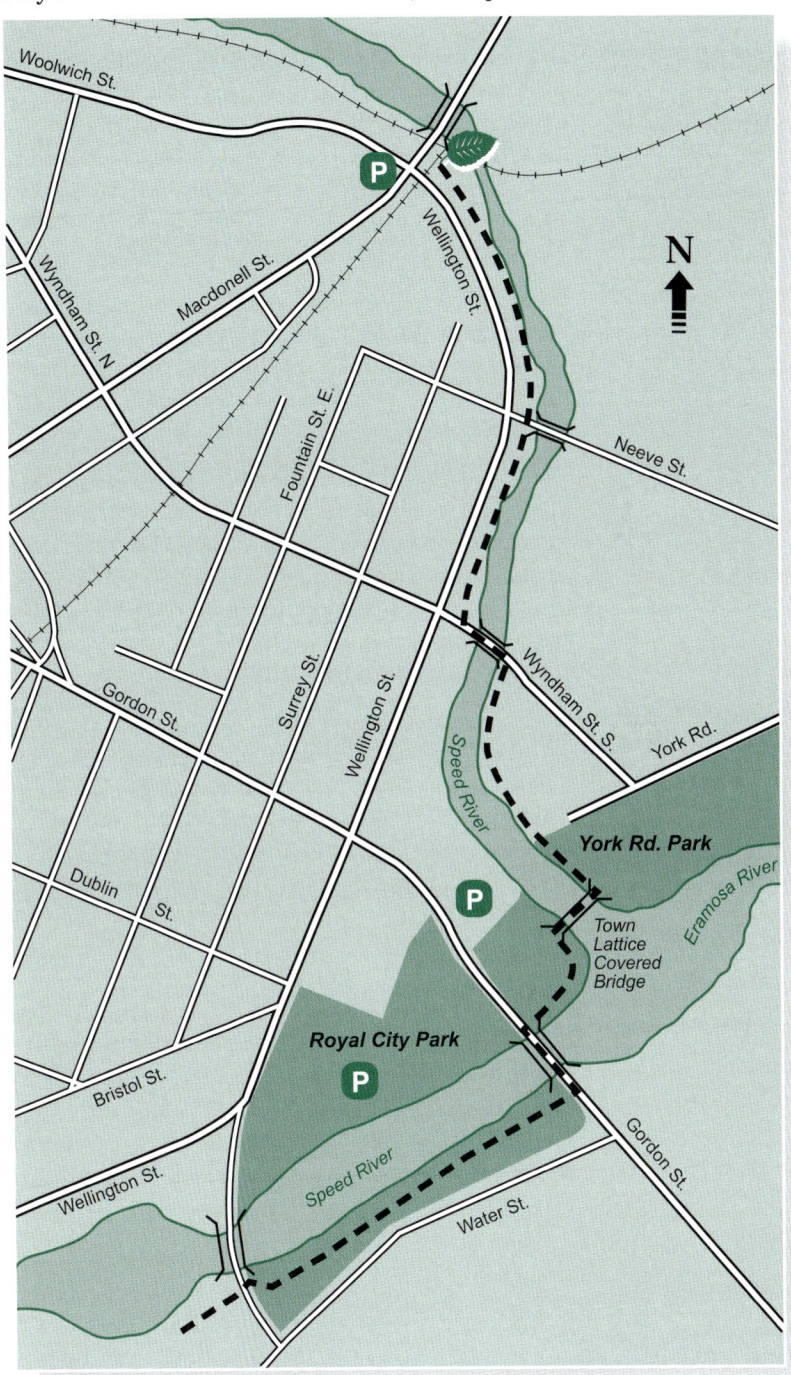

Ruthven Riverside Trail, Cayuga

- 2 km loop

- Beginner

Within the Grand River watershed sits a Greek revival style stone mansion nestled in a 1,500- acre Carolinian forest. You can see it from the water's edge on the Riverside Trail, perched on the hill. This National Historic Site was modeled on a 19th century English country estate and built in the 1840s by David Thompson, the contractor who built the original Welland Canal, and promoter of the Grand River Canal.

Forming part of the North Cayuga Slough Forest and wetlands, this area is rich in wildlife. More than 400 different plant species have been identified by naturalists, including ten provincially endangered plants. Bird banding studies are also currently under way. But the trail is also rich in history.

The trail starts from the mansion and passes stone ruins on the way to the river. Other than the steep grades to and from the river, it is a pleasant walk. Toward the end of the trail you'll pass the Thompson Family Cemetery, the coach house stables and the Barracks, or Drill Hall, built in 1867, before returning to the mansion. The mansion and its contents remain much the same as it did when the Thompsons owned the estate. It is open for tours on specific days.

A Greek Revival style stone masion within a 1,500 acre Carolinian forest

Ruthven has a number of outdoor trails, including the Carolinian Woodland Trail and the Indiana Trail, but the Riverside Trail is most suited for spring hiking as it is less muddy. If you want a longer walk, the 250 km Grand Valley Trail crosses through the Ruthven property for about two kilometers of its route.

TRAIL SURFACE: Hard-packed earth.

IF YOU GO: From Brantford, take Highway 403 to the Garden Avenue/Cainsville exit and travel south to a left turn onto Highway 54. Ruthven is on your right-hand side between York and Cayuga. Ruthven's phone is (905) 772-0560 and an admission fee applies for mansion tours. Hikers can park at the gatehouse in the daytime if the gate is closed.

Ruthven Riverside Trail, Cayuga

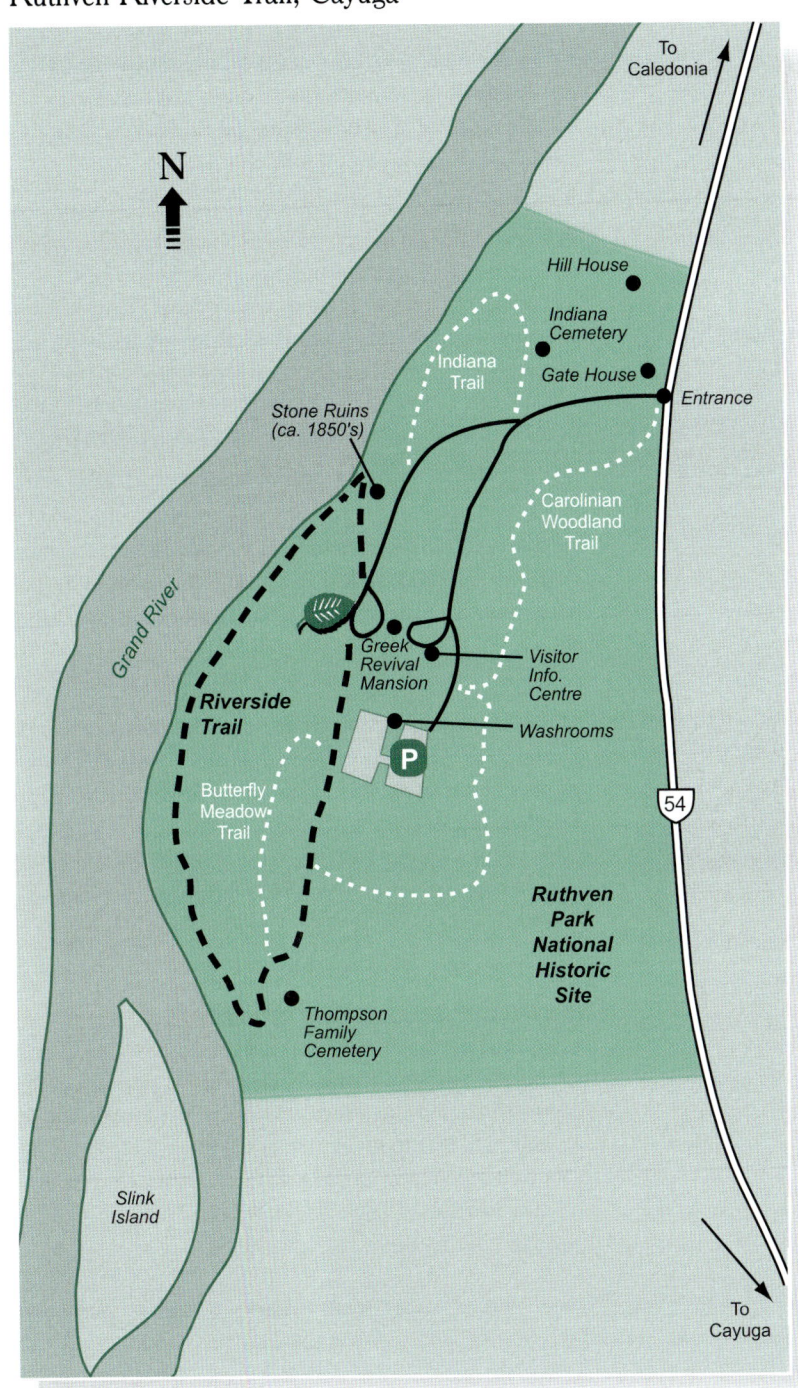

N

To Caledonia

Hill House

Indiana Cemetery

Indiana Trail

Gate House

Entrance

Stone Ruins (ca. 1850's)

Carolinian Woodland Trail

Grand River

Greek Revival Mansion

Visitor Info. Centre

Riverside Trail

Washrooms

Butterfly Meadow Trail

P

Ruthven Park National Historic Site

54

Thompson Family Cemetery

Slink Island

To Cayuga

S.C. Johnson Trail, Paris to Brantford

- 11 km

- Beginner

The S.C. Johnson Trail links the Cambridge to Paris Rail-trail with the Hamilton to Brantford Rail-Trail and Brantford's Gordon Glaves Memorial Pathway, to form a continuous route from Cambridge to Hamilton.

Part of the Trans Canada Trail system, the entire 11 kilometre stretch is worth traveling for the views at the beginning and end of the trail. You ride above Paris, looking down on rooftops, the CN railway bridge and the Grand River as it sweeps through the town. At the Brantford end, the trail towers over the Grand River along the edge of a steep embankment. It's one of the most picturesque spots along the Grand as it curves around part of Brant Conservation Area.

Be careful when crossing Curtis Avenue and the former Highway 2 in Paris, as this is a busy intersection. After the crossing, the trail continues at the top of the hill. For a detailed map, be sure to pick up a brochure at the trail kiosk in Paris, or print one from the GRCA website at www.grandriver.ca.

There is a mixture of nature and industry along this trail. You'll cross a former railway bridge over Highway 403 and pass new industrial areas. Mixed in with these sights are farm pastures, old apple trees and geese along the riverbank. Near the start of the trail in Paris, stop at a cemetery on your left-hand side just south of the CNR overpass. In it you'll find many old gravestones from the 1800s, including one of Hiram Capron, founder of Paris. And remember the views at the beginning and end of the trail are worth the ride.

One of the most picturesque spots along the Grand

TRAIL SURFACE: Stone dust.

IF YOU GO: From Highway 401, take the Highway 24 South exit and drive through Cambridge. Turn right on East River Road through Glen Morris into Paris. As you enter the town, you'll see parking at the Jean Rich Foundation Trailhead on your right-hand side or at the end of Power Line Road approximately midway along the trail. In Brantford, you can park on Dufferin Avenue or Parkside Drive. (There is limited parking at the Wilkes Dam Trailhead).

S.C. Johnson Trail, Paris to Brantford

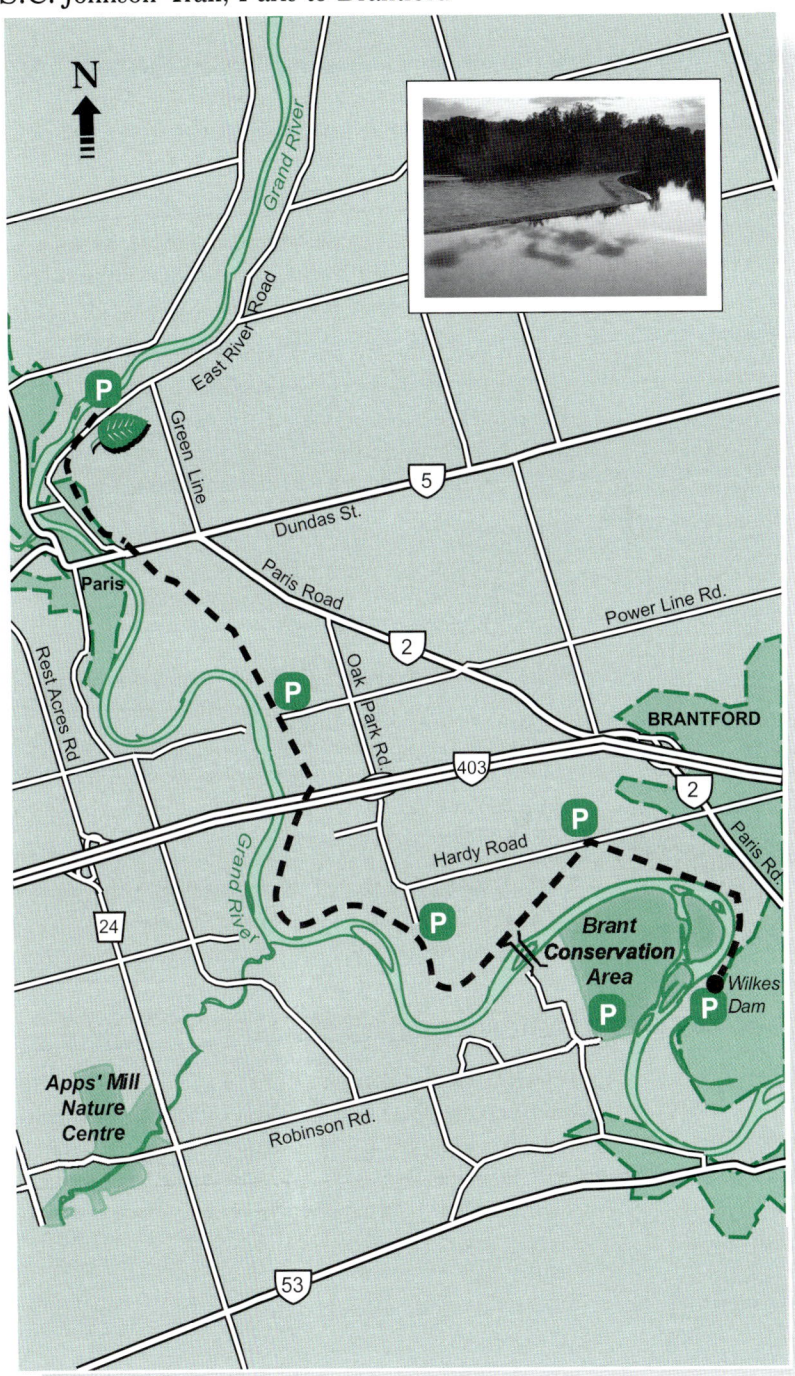

Schneider's Greenway Trail, Kitchener

- 2.5 km linear
- Beginner

Next time you walk through crowds of people at Fairview Mall, head to Schneider's Greenway afterward. Adjacent to Homer Watson Park, it's a natural retreat from walls of concrete and tiled floors, and a wonderful retreat on a warm winter day.

The small green space runs along Schneider's Creek, a tributary of the Grand River. Bordered by trees, the path also passes a playground and baseball diamond mid-way.

Even on warm days, the trail still bears signs of a long winter. The dried heads of thistles and Queen Anne's lace are capped with snow. Numerous branches and trunks show bare patches, gnawed by rabbits and deer. Maple keys still wave on a branch, the edges tattered by harsh winter winds.

Although the trail is still covered with snow, there are signs of spring. The creek is full of water and gurgling. The music of songbirds accompanies the distant sound of traffic. And then there are the hidden indicators.

A shaft of goldenrod bears the coming of spring

On a long shaft of goldenrod, a dark growth the size of a walnut bears the coming of spring. A goldenrod gallfly is over-wintering in this lair. As the weather warms, the larva will eat its way out of this shell and burst into spring. So will the buds on the trees and shrubs. So will the plants that are starting their long climb toward the surface.

The Schneider's Greenway Trail eventually runs into Manitou Drive. If you want a longer walk, cross Wabanaki and walk in the other direction. You'll eventually enter Homer Watson Park.

TRAIL SURFACE: Pavement.

IF YOU GO: From Highway 401, take Highway 8 north to Kitchener. Exit at the Fairway Road exit, turn right on King Street East and then right on Fairway Road. From Fairway Road, turn south (left) on Manitou Drive and then left onto Wabanaki Drive. There is a parking lot off Wabanaki at Kevco Place. Other parking is available on side streets or in Homer Watson Park.

Schneider's Greenway Trail, Kitchener

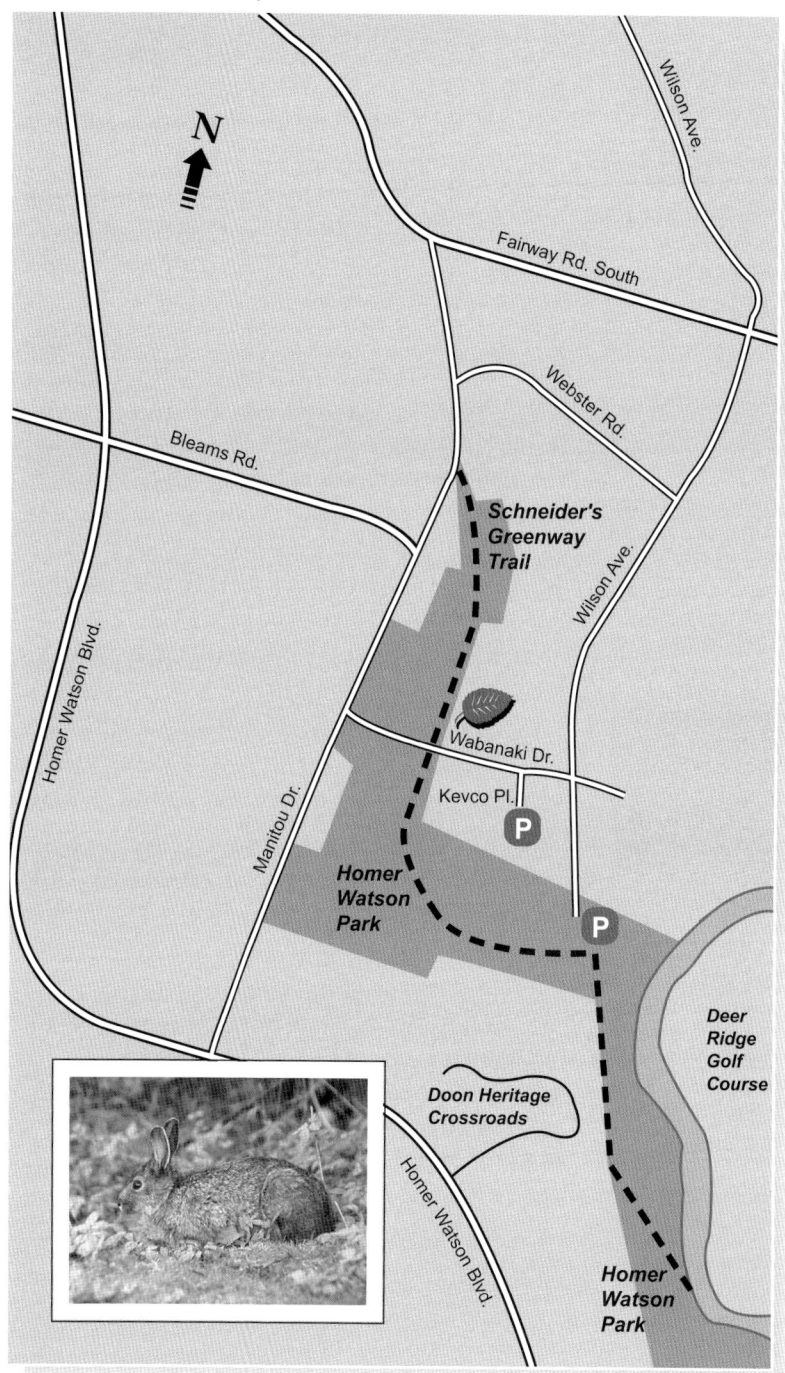

Shade's Mills Trail, Cambridge

- 14 km loop (Other Area Trails: interconnected loops)

- Beginner

Located on the eastern edge of the City of Cambridge, Shade's Mills Conservation Area has a series of interconnected loop trails along with a sandy beach, swimming area and picnic spots.

The start of the trail follows the Shade's Mills reservoir and then continues along Mill Creek, on the newly built Toyota Way Trail. There are various openings to the creek to allow close-up views of the water.

From the creek, you'll pass a tree mosaic as you walk deeper into the forest. A variety of pines as well as shagbark hickory, basswood and white ash can be seen. The best time to spot the resident family of white-tailed deer is early in the morning when they move from bedding areas to feeding spots near the water.

After crossing Mill Creek on the footbridge, follow the map closely because there are many loops to choose from. They enter forested areas and pass through meadows where tall grasses border the path and daisies, thimbleweed, buttercup and bladder campion bloom in the fields.

At the northeast end of the loop, a trail leads down to Mill Creek, a great spot for brown trout fishing. In the 36-hectare (89-acre) reservoir, swim northern pike, perch and large and smallmouth bass.

A great spot for fishing

TRAIL SURFACE: Wood mulch, stone dust, hard-packed earth and grass - groomed in winter for cross-country skiing.

IF YOU GO: From Highway 401 heading east from Kitchener to Cambridge, take the Franklin Boulevard exit. Turn left on Avenue Road. Shade's Mills is on the right. From Highway 401 heading west from Guelph, take the Townline Road exit. Turn left/south onto Townline Road. Turn right on Avenue Road and Shade's Mills is on the left. The park phone number is (519) 621-3697 and an admission fee applies in season.

Shade's Mills Trail, Cambridge

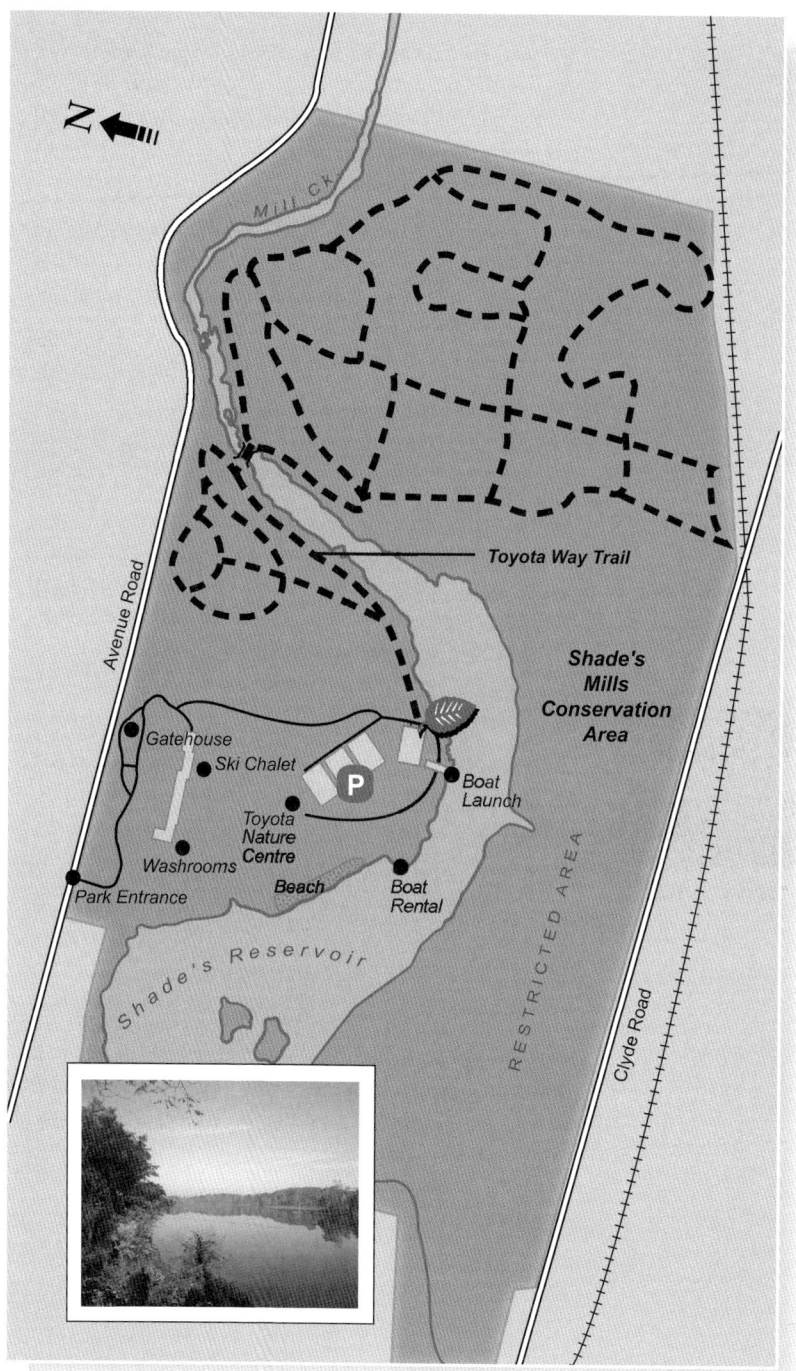

Silver Lake Trail, Waterloo

- 2 km loop
- Beginner

Can you remember summer days when we've experienced cold weather? If you walk the Silver Lake Trail, you'll be consoled that you didn't miss out. In 1816, our region had an unusual summer with nightly frosts that continued into the month of July.

It was during this summer that Abraham Erb's gristmill was built. Farmers were eager to earn extra money because their crops weren't growing well. A replica of the mill stands at the head of Silver Lake and the Interpretive History Walk has a number of placards that explain the historical significance.

From the gristmill, follow the Silver Lake boardwalk out to the lookout and pavilions. The trail skirts the lake and then a wooded area across from the petting zoo.

Follow the trail across the bridge over the lake where it connects with the Trans Canada Trail if you want a longer walk. When the Grand Trunk Railway came to Waterloo in 1886, it bought a right-of-way across the millpond from William Snider. When the millpond was sold in 1917, a pedestrian walkway was built alongside the railway tracks so people could reach Waterloo Park.

A replica of the mill stands at the head of Silver Lake

As you walk toward the end of the trail, you'll notice areas filled with water lilies and other aquatic plants. Planted by volunteers, they help purify the water. Also take note of the last placard that has some interesting information about Silver Lake being a source for ice until modern refrigeration arrived in the 1920s.

TRAIL SURFACE: Hard-packed earth, gravel, grass, boardwalk.

IF YOU GO: From the Conestoga Parkway, take the University Avenue West exit, turn left onto Seagram Drive and park in the Waterloo Park parking lot. Walk past the zoo and you'll see Silver Lake in the corner. Alternatively, you can park at the Waterloo Public Library, or in the parking lot at Erb Street and Father David Bauer Drive.

Silver Lake Trail, Waterloo

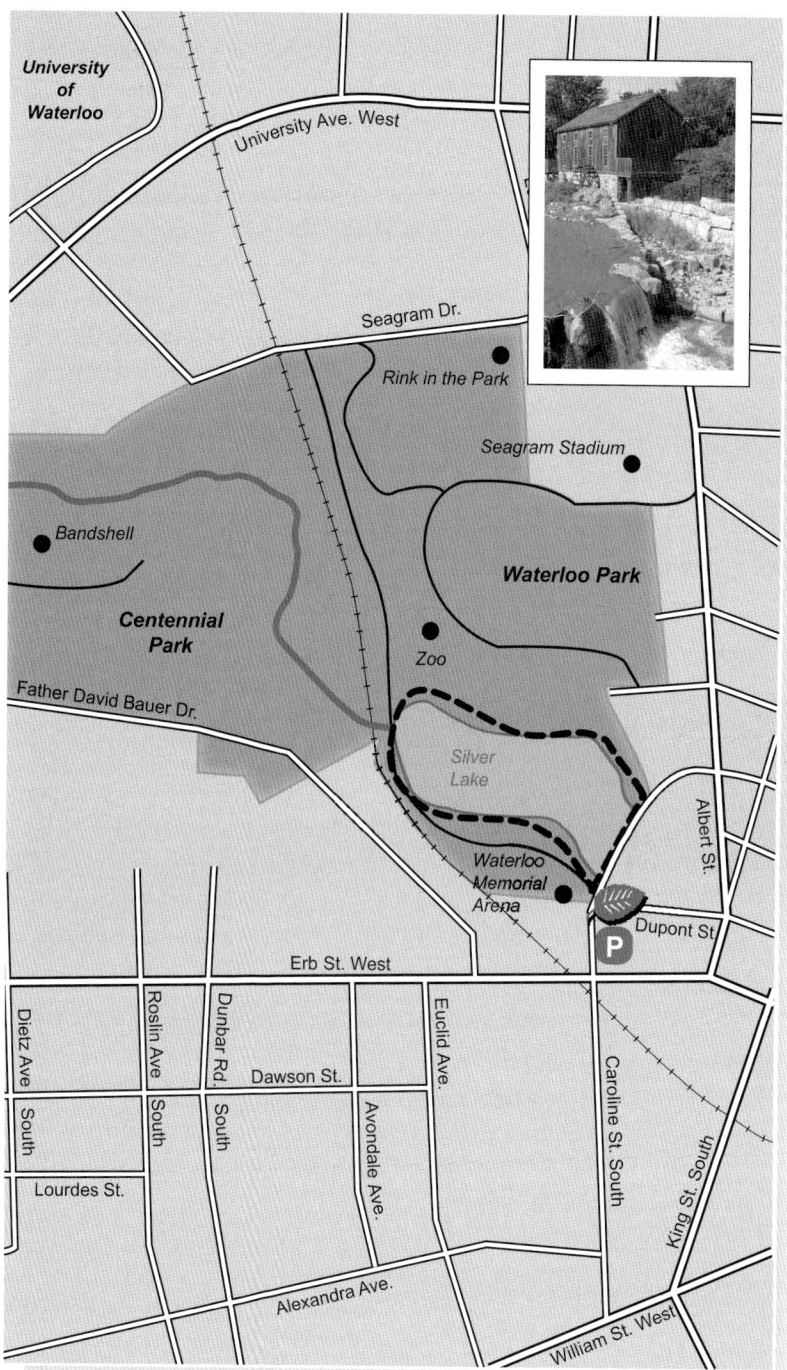

University of Waterloo

University Ave. West

Seagram Dr.

Rink in the Park

Seagram Stadium

Bandshell

Waterloo Park

Centennial Park

Zoo

Father David Bauer Dr.

Silver Lake

Waterloo Memorial Arena

Albert St.

Dupont St.

P

Erb St. West

Dietz Ave

Roslin Ave

Dunbar Rd.

South

South

South

Dawson St.

Euclid Ave.

Avondale Ave.

Caroline St. South

King St. South

Lourdes St.

Alexandra Ave.

William St. West

Speed River Trail, Guelph

- 3.4 km linear
- Beginner

Most people know Riverside Park by its floral clock, but there is a trail that runs along the river where fall colours reflect in the water, benches await at scenic spots and nature offers its own unique vantage points.

The trail starts within Riverside Park and follows the east side of the Speed River, passing the Dutch Mill and crossing the river over the suspension bridge. If you're travelling with children, the playground is a welcome stop along the way.

The trail continues north to Woodlawn Road. When you cross the road, the pathway continues slightly to your right and enters a natural area. You walk through cedar lowlands, with a glimpse of the river before heading into the woodlands and behind a residential area.

When this leaf-strewn pathway makes a sharp left turn, you'll cross a bridge over a stream and head toward the river and its woodlands. The trail makes a few sharp turns along with the river, offering glimpses through the trees of side trails that lead to the water's edge. Make sure you follow one of these, walking toward the sound of water pooling and pushing through and around rocks.

Otherwise you'll see the river through the trees. In a cedar lowland, the lack of undergrowth draws attention to the large trees, their wide bases branching into two or more separate trunks that rise tall into the sky.

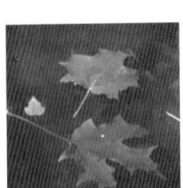

Fall colours reflect in the water

This trail ends at Victoria Road, and although you return on the same pathway, the river and its surroundings will look new from this perspective.

TRAIL SURFACE: Stone dust, hard-packed earth, some pavement.

IF YOU GO: From Highway 401, take Highway 6 North toward Guelph. Turn right on Speedvale Avenue. Cross over Woolwich Street and turn left onto Riverview Drive. Parking will be on your immediate left.

please feel free to return it for refund or exchange within 14 days; we simply ask that the item be returned in store-bought condition and be accompanied by a proof of purchase from any of our stores. Items accompanied by a gift receipt and returned in store-bought condition may be exchanged or refunded onto a credit note for the value of the item at the time of purchase. Please note we cannot provide an exchange or refund of magazines or newspapers.

Si vous n'êtes pas entièrement satisfait d'un de vos achats, n'hésitez pas à le retourner pour un remboursement ou un échange dans un délai de 14 jours. Nous exigeons cependant que l'article soit dans le même état qu'au moment de l'achat et que vous présentiez un reçu provenant d'une de nos librairies. Les articles accompagnés d'un reçu-cadeau et retournés en condition de revente peuvent être échangés ou remboursés par une note de crédit pour la valeur de l'article lors de l'achat. Veuillez noter qu'aucun échange ou remboursement ne sera accepté pour les magazines ou les journaux.

If, for any reason, you purchase an item that is not totally satisfactory, please feel free to return it for refund or exchange within 14 days; we simply ask that the item be returned in store-bought condition and be accompanied by a proof of purchase from any of our stores. Items accompanied by a gift receipt and returned in store-bought condition may be exchanged or refunded onto a credit note for the value of the item at the time of purchase. Please note we cannot provide an exchange or refund of magazines or newspapers.

Si vous n'êtes pas entièrement satisfait d'un de vos achats, n'hésitez pas à le retourner pour un remboursement ou un échange dans un délai de 14 jours. Nous exigeons cependant que l'article soit dans le même état qu'au moment de l'achat et que vous présentiez un reçu provenant d'une de nos librairies. Les articles accompagnés d'un reçu-cadeau et retournés en condition de revente peuvent être échangés ou remboursés par une note de crédit pour la valeur de l'article lors de l'achat. Veuillez

Chapters

Store# 00780 Chapters Guelph
Stone Road Mall,
435 Stone Road West
Guelph,ON N1G 2X6
Phone: (519) 766-9122

You could win $1000 or an iPod!
Complete our survey at
www.indigofeedback.com
or call 1-866-379-4970.
See site for contest rules.
Store# 00780 Term# 004 Trans# 266462

TRANSACTION RECORD
INTERAC DIRECT PAYMENT

Card Number : ************7002
Account   : DEBIT CARD
Account Type : CHEQUING
Trans Type   : PURCHASE
Amount   : $20.95
Merchant ID : 040080030651
Terminal #   : 004   Operator : 704
Date   : 06/06/2009 Time   : 13:05:16
Auth #   : 471301   Bank Ref : 00000036
                APPROVED

***** CUSTOMER COPY *****

Speed River Trail, Guelph

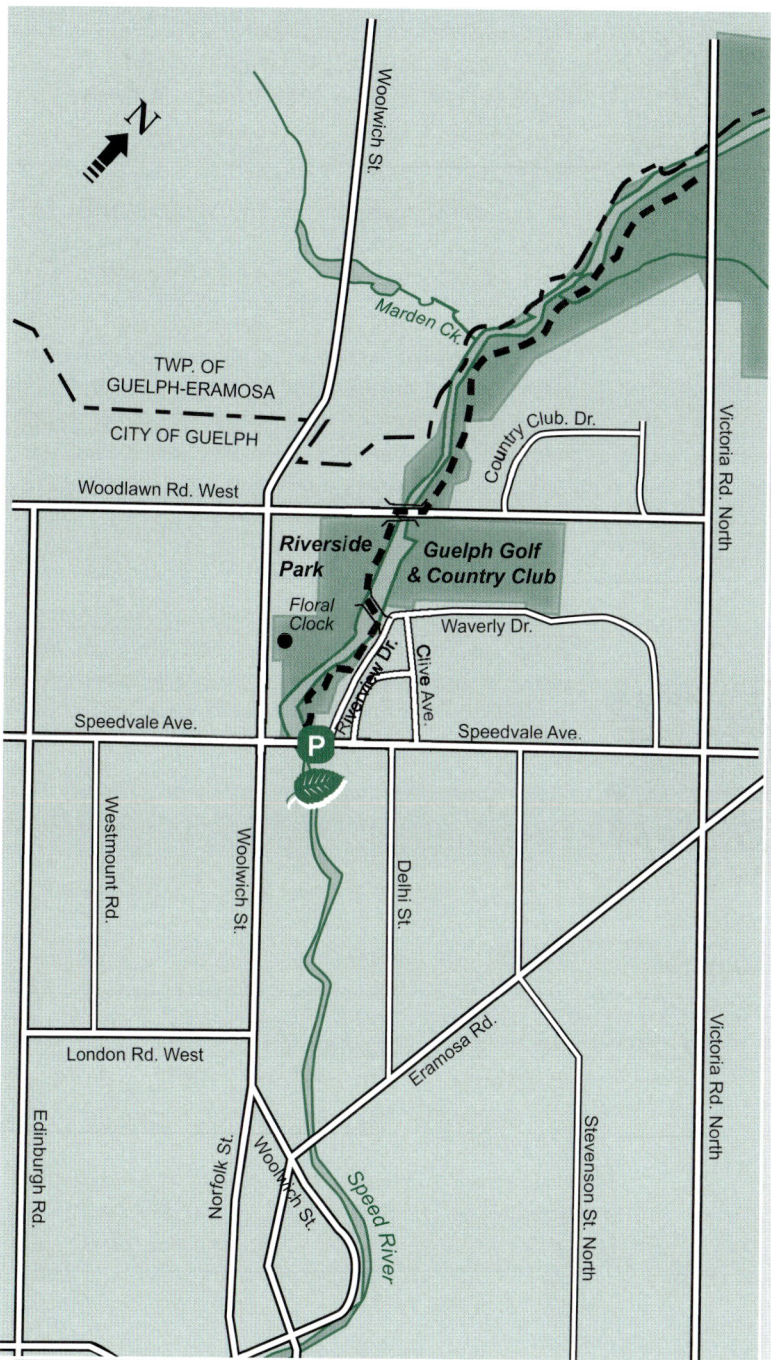

Taquanyah Nature Centre Trail, Cayuga

- 2.7 km loop (yellow trail)
- Beginner

This trail wanders through many habitats, from coldwater stream and marsh to a rare Carolinian forest. Depending on the season, your attention will be drawn from wild rose bushes to tulip trees and quail to ruffed grouse.

The trail starts by passing a spring fed pond and bluebird birdhouses and then winds through open prairie grasslands where you might hear the meadowlark's clear, mellow whistle.

When you round the corner around the eastern white pine plantation, the Carolinian forest appears on your left. This is a rare temperate zone that contains plants and animals typically found farther south in the United States. You'll see the Red Trail on your left that leads through the Carolinian forest where burr oak and shagbark hickory are among the unique tree species you'll see. This area is also a protected habitat for warblers and other Carolinian Species. It's extremely important to stay on the marked trail and not disturb this area in any way. This woodland trail has many scenic turns from the boardwalk around the pond, white trilliums along the forest floor in springtime, and the rare spotting of a salamander near wetland areas.

You'll find different Carolinian species throughout the property, such as Persimon and American Chestnut trees behind the nature centre.

You'll find different Carolinian species

TRAIL SURFACE: Hard-packed earth, grass, boardwalk.

IF YOU GO: From Brantford, take Highway 403 to the Garden Avenue/Cainsville exit and travel south to Highway 54. Turn left and proceed south through Caledonia and York. Turn right on Regional Road 9 in York. After crossing the Grand River, turn left on River Road and in a few kilometres, turn right on Townline Road. You'll see Taquanyah on your left-hand side.

Taquanyah Nature Centre Trail, Cayuga

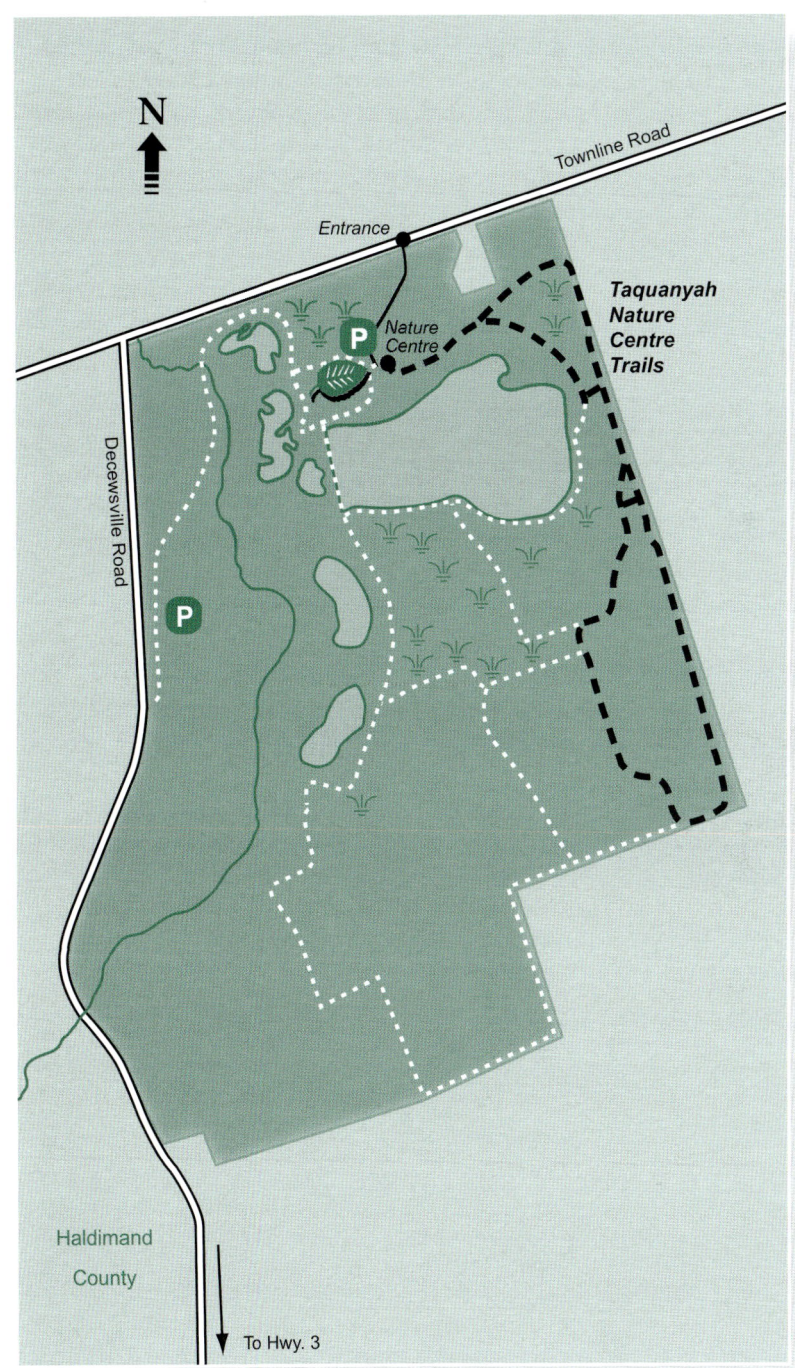

N

Townline Road

Entrance

P Nature Centre

Taquanyah Nature Centre Trails

Decewsville Road

P

Haldimand County

To Hwy. 3

Victoria Woods Trail, Guelph

- 2 km loop
- Beginner

At Victoria Woods, white trilliums sit at the feet of old-growth trees, blanketing the ground. The trail passes ponds and a thick canopy of sugar maple, white ash, black cherry and beech. From these treetops you'll hear the red-eyed vireo sing, its musical call ringing through the treetops, even when it's hot.

Trilliums are found throughout hardwood forests in the spring, but there are few spots in the region that are blessed with such thick pockets of these delicate flowers. Victoria Woods is one of them.

Often growing near trilliums you'll spot the speckled leaves of the Trout Lily (Erythronium americanum), also known as Dogtooth Violet. Please note that wildflowers should not be picked. They wilt within a few hours if placed in a vase and they don't transplant well when taken out of woodland conditions.

The trail ends at the J. C. Taylor Nature Centre and Gosling Wildlife Gardens, which is also full of wildlife as well as many blooming flowerbeds. If you want a longer walk, the Victoria Woods trail connects to the 1.1 km Ivey Trail.

TRAIL SURFACE: Wood chips, hard-packed earth.

IF YOU GO: From Highway 401, take the Hanlon Expressway/Highway 6 North to Guelph. Turn right on Stone Road and after passing Gordon Street, turn left into the University of Guelph and follow signs for the Arboretum. 519-824-4120 for the Guelph Arboretum.

White trilliums sit at the feet of old-growth trees

Victoria Woods Trail, Guelph

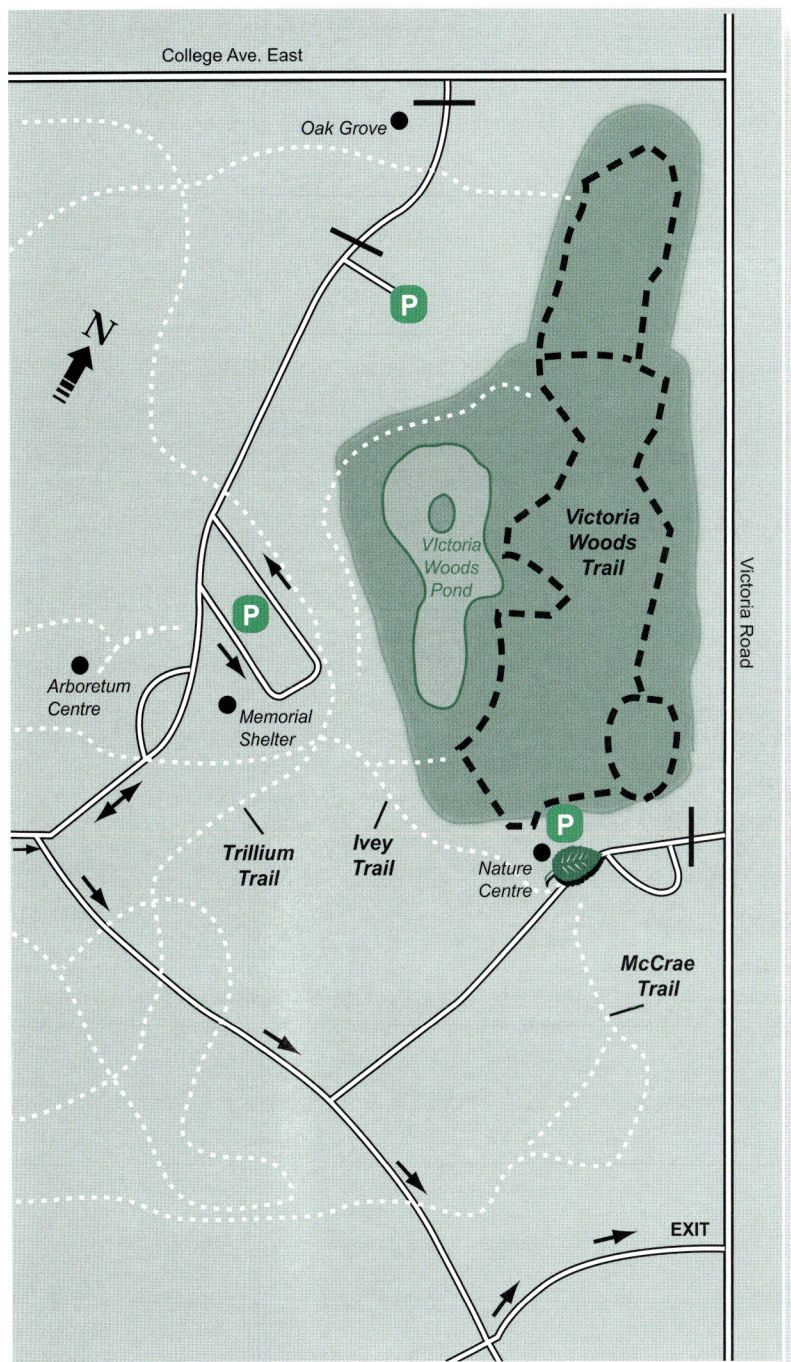

Walter Bean Trail:
Economical Insurance Trailway, Waterloo

- 2.5 km linear

- Beginner

The first early winter scene to greet you on this trail is a stand of snow-covered thistles, some more than four feet tall with snow resting in them like honey in a comb. The pathway then leads to the river's edge, where you cross a bridge over a stream before heading into the forest.

As you wind through the woodland and cross over a deeper valley, logs and downed saplings lie suspended above the ground. Yet the snow highlights each of them in shape, texture and colour -- smooth smoky grey beech and thin dark green cedar.

The forest sections in this trail are never far from the river. Even when surrounded by trees, you can hear the geese calling from the open waters, the familiar sound of fall that enters winter.

You'll emerge on a high riverbank and follow the trail by an old ruin topped with snow, before dipping into a cedar forest. You'll walk into a high bank view again, this time with a bench overlooking a bend in the river.

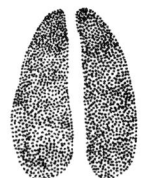

Windswept banks reveal animal tracks that lead to the river's edge

This trail comes out behind the maintenance yard parking lot behind Bingemans. Follow the signs and continue to Marshall Hall. Then follow the sign on the hydro pole in front of Marshall Hall that points in the direction of the mini golf course area. Continue walking on the road and you'll come to the water park area and see the kiosk for the trail.

TRAIL SURFACE: Stone dust, gravel.

IF YOU GO: From Victoria Street, turn left onto Lancaster Street West and right onto Wellington Street North. Turn left onto Riverbend Drive and you'll see the trail kiosk and parking area on your right just past the Humane Society.

Walter Bean Trail: Economical Insurance Trailway, Waterloo

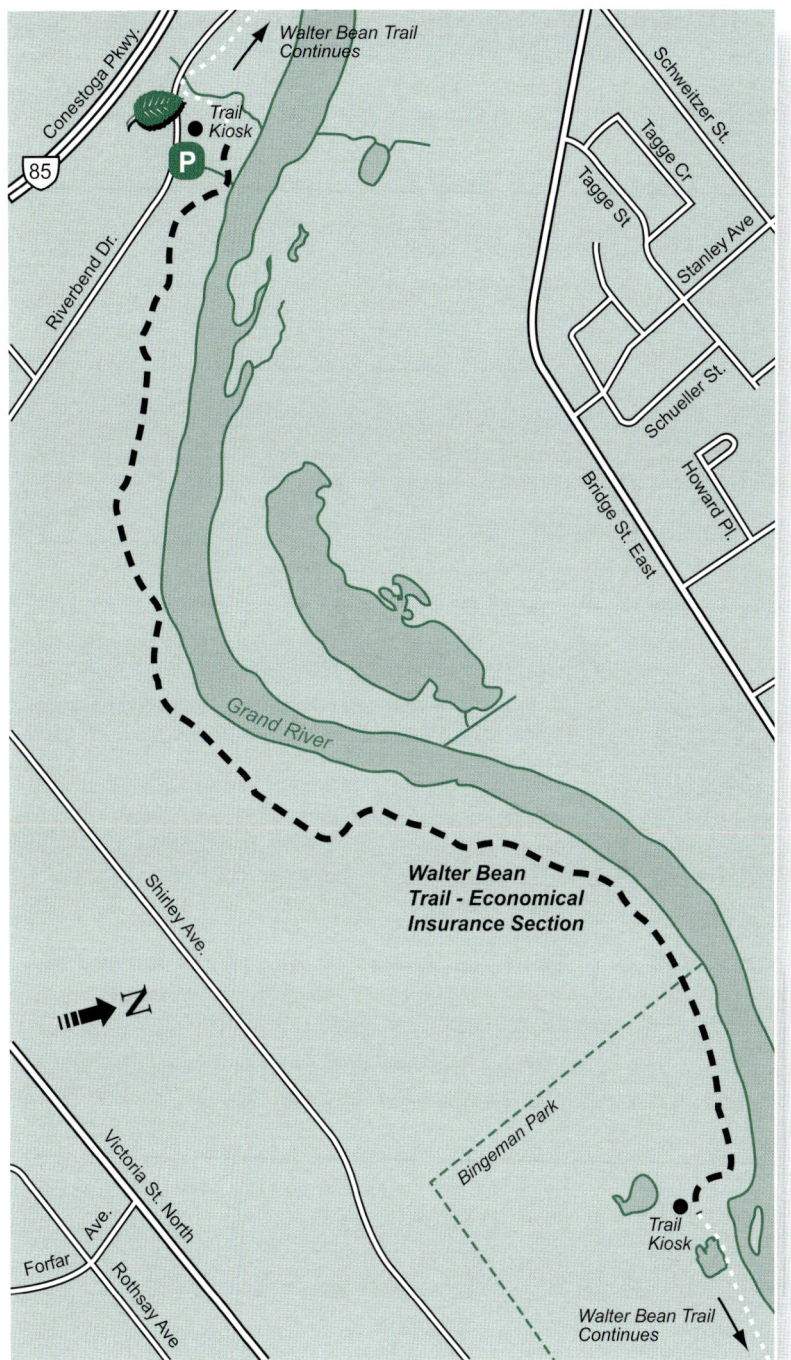

Walter Bean Trail:
J.A. Pollock Family Trailway, Kitchener

- 2.5 km linear
- Beginner

You'll emerge on a high river bank before dipping into a cedar forest

If you stand back and look at tree trunks, you'll notice colour variations of chocolate brown, tan and russet, but you can also see designs on the trunks. Different shapes and figures emerge depending on how snow has collected in the bark. In between grooves, loose bark and forks where branches reach out, snow acts like a paintbrush highlighting the different features.

This trail leaves the traffic noise of Highway 7 to squeeze between two ponds before turning a bend left toward the river. At one point, you'll walk behind an industrial area by Victoria Street, before descending to the river. Other than this, the river is the focus. Geese float on the open water. Windswept banks reveal animal tracks that lead to the river's edge.

Wildlife tracks are more common if you head out after a fresh snowfall. The heart-shaped pointed print of a deer is common in woodland areas. But also look for the tiny patterns such as mice tracks that suddenly disappear into a snowbank. Below an insulating blanket of snow, shrews, moles and mice may be scurrying through an underground passageway.

After following the river for a while, the trail gradually descends into Bingeman Park. Cedar trees lean in to create a canopy over you. Brown tufts of dry grasses stick out of the snow on the opposite riverbank. Snowcapped goldenrods edge the trail.

The trail passes through the campground spaces and then enters the picnic area. It eventually comes out near the Glen Pavilion Area and playfield. Walk toward the Walter Bean kiosk at the parking lot for the end of the trail.

TRAIL SURFACE: Stone dust, gravel.

IF YOU GO: From Victoria Street (Highway 7), pass Bingemans and continue driving toward Guelph. Turn left on Shirley Drive (before the Grand River bridge) and park in the Stanley Park Optimist Natural Area parking lot. You can also park at Bingeman Park and start from the Walter Bean kiosk.

Walter Bean Trail: J.A. Pollock Family Trailway, Kitchener

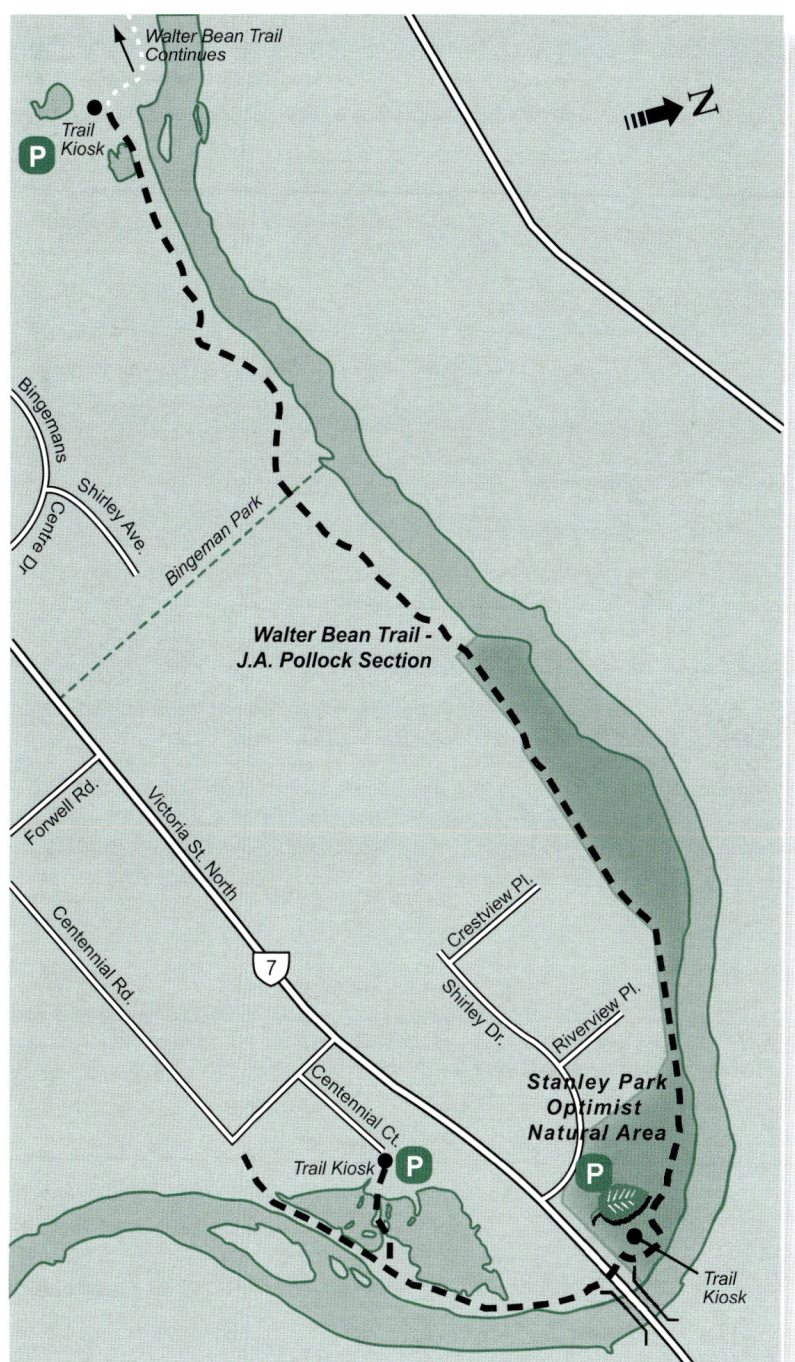

Walter Bean Trail
Continues

Trail
Kiosk

N

Bingemans
Centre Dr.

Shirley Ave.

Bingeman Park

**Walter Bean Trail -
J.A. Pollock Section**

Forwell Rd.

Victoria St. North

Centennial Rd.

7

Crestview Pl.

Shirley Dr.

Riverview Pl.

Centennial Ct.

Trail Kiosk

**Stanley Park
Optimist
Natural Area**

Trail
Kiosk

Walter Bean Trailhead, Cambridge

• 2 km linear
• Beginner

The Walter Bean trailhead is an important part of Cambridge's Grand Trunk Trail and combines with the Trans Canada Trail at this point.

From the George Street parking lot, you look down a long pathway covered by a canopy of trees. This is the beauty of rail-trails - long straight pathways that are simple to follow.

This walk leads you through part of the Cruickston Park Environmentally Sensitive Policy Area (E.S.P.A.) as designated by the Region of Waterloo, as the trail runs along the western bank of the Grand River. Although most of the river is hidden behind the forest you walk through, you can catch more glimpses of the river upon returning if you continue on the trail along the limestone bluffs. If you head toward Riverbluffs Park, you'll walk along the river for a stretch.

When you leave the forested area you'll come onto a paved section that runs parallel with Blair Road. Even though you are merged with traffic, nature still surrounds you. Cattails and bulrushes border the wetland, and tall woodlands from Cruickston Park contrast the golden crop fields on your right where the trees border the river's edge.

Continue onto the Blair Trail and end on Fountain Street at The Record Heritage Trailpoint. More than $30,000, raised from the sale of the first Grand River Country Trails book, helped build the trail and this kiosk.

Cattails and bulrushes border the wetland

TRAIL SURFACE: Stone dust and pavement.

IF YOU GO: From Highway 401, take Highway 8 south toward Cambridge. Turn right on Fountain Street and left on Waterloo Regional Road 42. After driving through the village of Blair, past Langdon Drive and countryside, take the left fork that turns into George Street in Cambridge (Galt). You'll see a parking lot on your left.

Walter Bean Trailhead, Cambridge

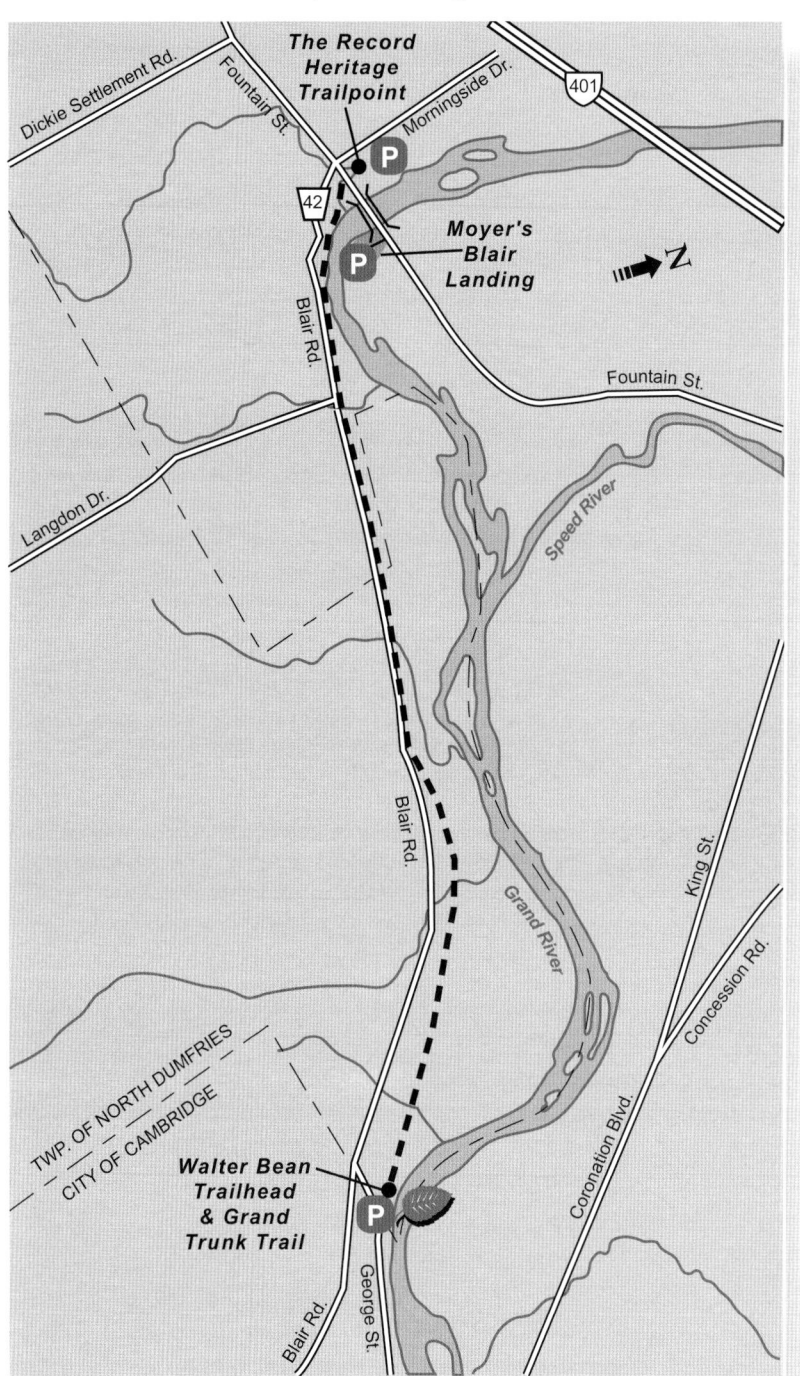

Woolwich Reservoir Elmira Lions Trail, Elmira

- 6.5 km loop
- Beginner

On a hot day this is a welcome trail, where much of the pathway is covered in shade, wind blows in strong from the water, and rest benches are tucked in among the cedars.

When facing the Woolwich Reservoir, turn to your left and take the trail that starts in the woods. You'll walk between a pine plantation and open fields where Queen Anne's lace and butterflies dance among the tall grasses. A cornfield will open on your left, and then more wildflowers: bright yellow buttercups, pink flower bunches hanging off the milkweed, deep purple vetch climbing up and winding around the trees.

Although you don't see the lake other than hints of blue peeking through the base of trees where needles have dried out, sidetrails lead to the water's edge. After you've crossed the bridge, you'll walk along the lake edge for a while. From the bridge you may have a chance to see the windsurfers who often frequent this lake. The next bridge crossing is near Floradale where you'll be able to stop in the park area where wandering geese, picnic tables and a playground offer a quiet break.

When you leave this mowed area, the trail becomes closed in by a canopy of trees. They form an alcove covered by evergreen boughs where light beckons you at the end of the straight pathway.

On a hot day this is a welcome trail

There is a short walk along Florapine Road for a while. But don't be dismayed at the lack of sights - there was more than one Mennonite buggy that passed on this road. At the top of the hill you'll see a gate on your right that leads back to the trail and passes through a mature hardwood forest.

The trail emerges by the lake where you'll walk on top of the reservoir dam. This offers a wide sweeping view of the lake, and as you stand listening to waves lapping the rocks, you may hear an exclamation or two as one of the many fishermen reels in a catch.

TRAIL SURFACE: Mowed grass.

IF YOU GO: Take Highway 85 from Waterloo toward St. Jacobs and continue on into Elmira. Once you pass through town, turn left on Red Woods Drive/Twp. Road 12. You'll see an Elmira Lions Trail and the Emergency Number is 7224. Please put a donation in the honour box registration.

Woolwich Reservoir Elmira Lions Trail, Elmira

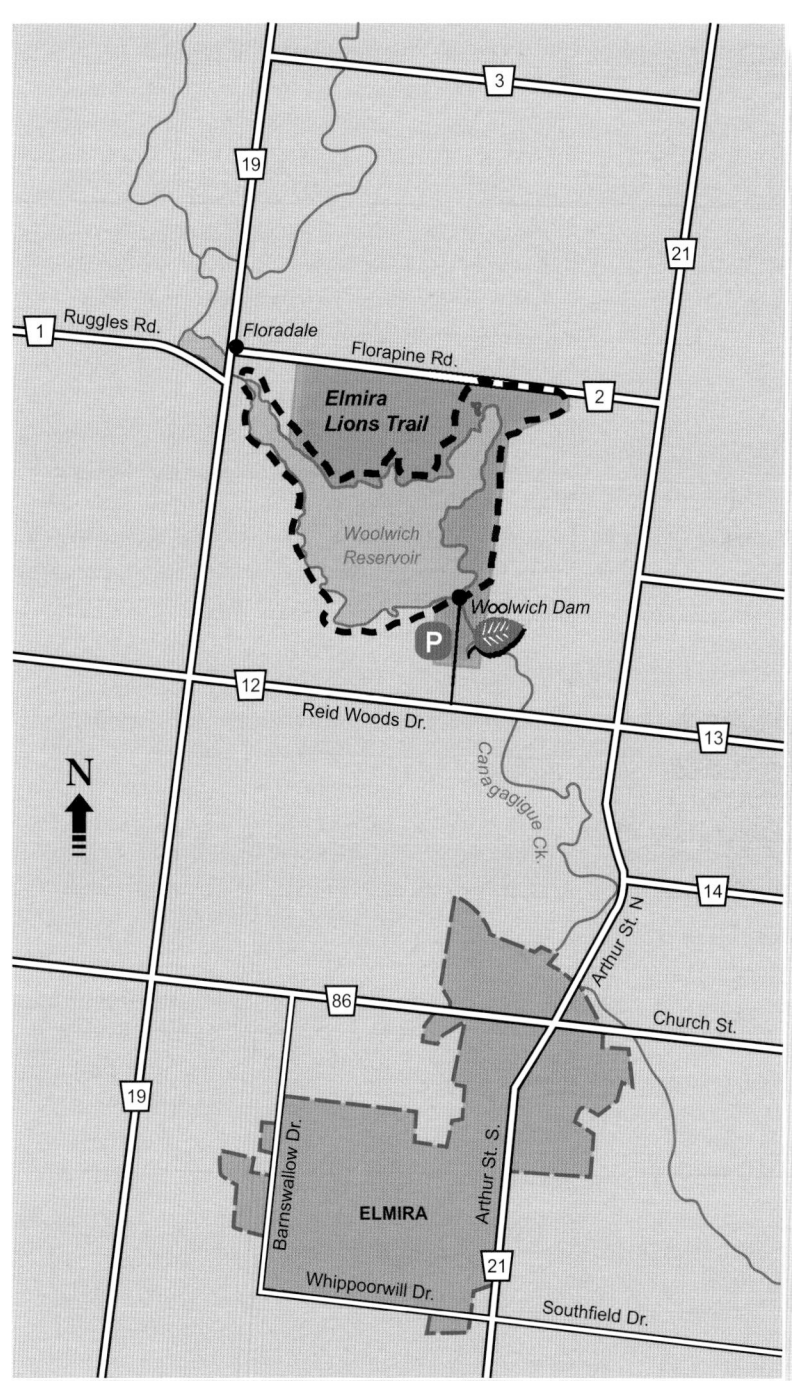

West Montrose Cycling Trail, West Montrose

- **17.1 km loop**
- **Beginner**

In 1881, the only traffic across the West Montrose covered bridge was horses and pedestrians. Today it's visited by people from the world over, crossing it on foot, horseback and bicycle, as well as by car. It's the only covered bridge left in Ontario.

This cycling route will take you across this historic bridge, past farm fields and along the Grand River. Start by cycling across the bridge where you'll hear your tires running over some of the walnut and maple wood that is substituted for the cedar shingles and oak floorboards used in this original structure. At one time, a two-centimetre gap was left between the boards so horse manure could fall through the cracks.

Although the bridge is now reinforced and has a speed and load limit, it retains trappings of times gone by. The electric lights resemble the lanterns that were hoisted onto a beam 18 feet above the bridge floor, and you'll still see old weathered boards and the sun shining through the planks.

It's the only covered bridge left in Ontario

From this bridge, there are many old country roads to cycle along. One option is to cross Highway 86 (beware of traffic on this busy road). From there continue on Woolwich Regional Road 62. You'll pass cows grazing in meadows, fields golden with crops and swallows perched on the hydro lines. You'll encounter a few rolling hills and will be happy to know when you turn right on 8th Line West, it's a flat road for a while. Turn right onto Regional Road 23 (this road has heavier traffic on weekends), cross Highway 86 again and turn right at Riverside Drive to return to the covered bridge.

Bike across the bridge again - you might see a Mennonite buggy passing through. Or cycle with a partner and stop in the middle of the bridge. It's known locally as the kissing bridge, so we'll leave the rest up to you!

TRAIL SURFACE: Pavement.

IF YOU GO: From Highway 86 travelling from Elmira toward Guelph, turn right on Regional Road 23 and right onto Rivers Edge Drive. Park near the picnic area.

West Montrose Cycling Trail, West Montrose

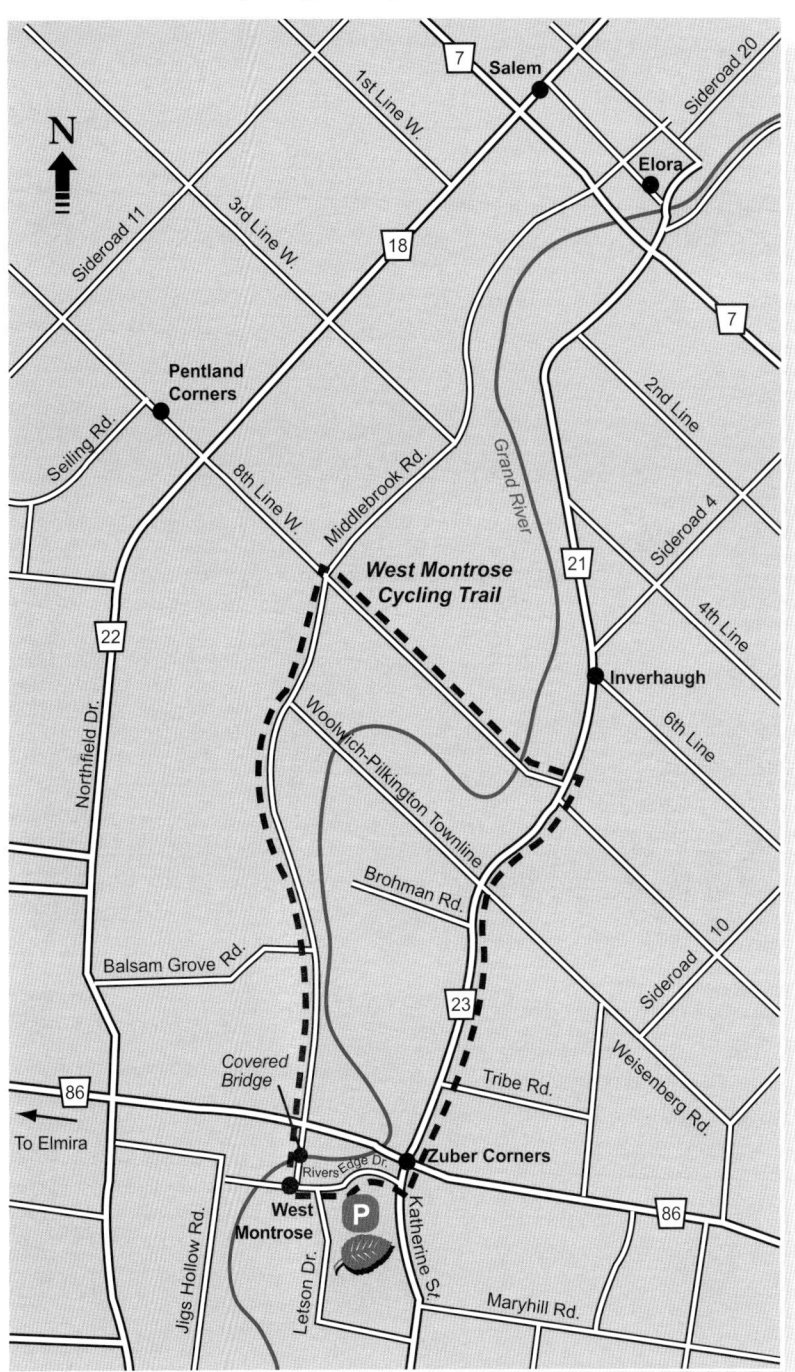

Animal Track Identification

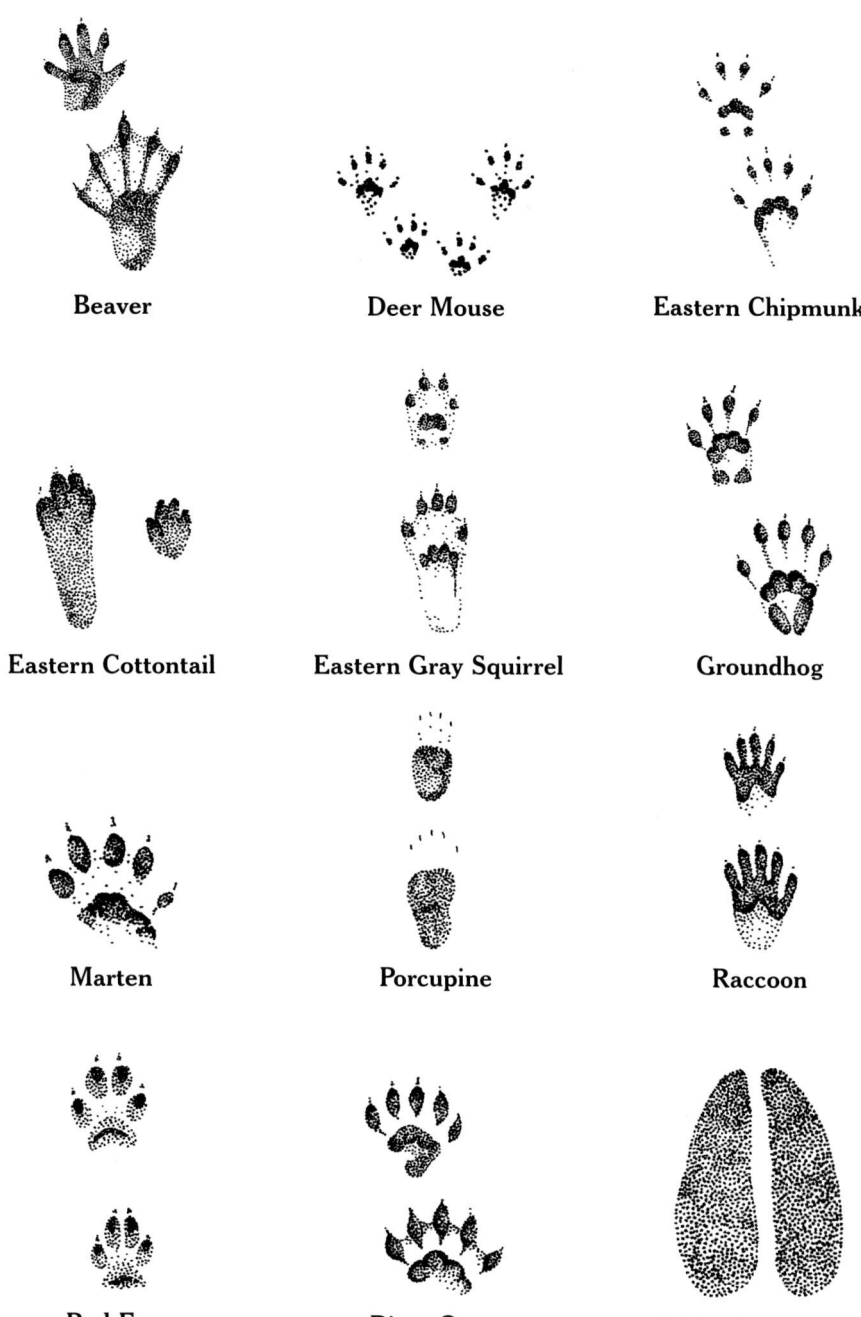

Beaver

Deer Mouse

Eastern Chipmunk

Eastern Cottontail

Eastern Gray Squirrel

Groundhog

Marten

Porcupine

Raccoon

Red Fox

River Otter

White-Tailed Deer

Spring Wildflower Identification

Bloodroot

Dutchman's Breeches

Marsh Marigold

May-apple

Spring Beauty

Trillium

Hepatica

Canada Violet

Trout Lily

Trail References

LONG-DISTANCE LINKS

The Grand Valley Trail

The Grand Valley Trail stretches for 250 kilometres (155 miles) from Rock Point Provincial Park on Lake Erie to the town of Alton near Orangeville.

Much of the trail follows the Grand River, with boardwalk, log bridge and stream crossings. It passes along cornfields, through old farm orchards and forests.

Grand Valley Trail Association,
75 King St. S.,
P.O. Box 40068,
RPO Waterloo Square,
Waterloo, Ont.   N2J 4V1
Website: www.gvta.on.ca

The Trans Canada Trail

Ontario trails make up about 20% of the total length of the 15,000 km (9,320 mile) Trans Canada Trail (TCT), Canada's coast-to-coast trail system.

Many of the trails in this book are part of the Trans Canada Trail, or provide linkages to it, to create the 3,000 km (1,864 miles) of trails that form Ontario's part of the Trans Canada Trail system.   These trails are still known by their local name, and are developed and maintained by local agencies or groups, but have registered to become part of the TCT network in southern Ontario.

Trans Canada Trail Foundation
43 Westminster Ave. N.
Montreal West, Quebec   H4X 1Y8
(800) 465-3636
Email: info@tctrail.ca
Website: www.tctrail.ca

The Walter Bean Grand River Trail

The existing trail is a partnership of the cities of Cambridge, Kitchener and Waterloo, and including the Region of Waterloo and Grand River Conservation Authority.

It follows the Grand River through most of Waterloo Region, with its construction funded by donations to the Walter Bean Grand River Community Trails Foundation.

Trail Information can be obtained from the cities, or by contacting:
Walter Bean Grand River Trail
11th floor Marsland Centre
20 Erb St. W.
Waterloo, Ontario   N2L 1T2
(519) 883-4104
Website: www.sju.ca/grt

TRIP PLANNING & TOURISM FOR GRAND RIVER COUNTRY

County of Brant
1-888-250-2296
www.brant.ca

Brantford Tourism
1-800-265-6299
www.brantford.ca/tourism

Cambridge Tourism
1-800-749-7560
www.cambridgetourism.com

Township of Woolwich
Visitor Information Centre
1-877-969-0094

Elora & Fergus Visitor Information
1-877-242-6353
www.ferguselora.com

**Grand River
Conservation Authority**
1-519-621-2761
www.grandriver.ca

Grand River Country
1-800-267-3399
www.grandrivercountry.com

Guelph Visitor Information Centre
1-800-334-4519
www.city.guelph.on.ca/visitor

Tourism Haldimand
1-800-863-9607
www.tourismhaldimand.com

**The Hills of Headwaters
Tourism Association**
1-800-332-9744
www.thehillsofheadwaters.com

Kitchener Waterloo Tourism
1-800-265-6959
www.kw-visitor.on.ca

**Ontario Ministry of
Tourism & Recreation**
1-800-668-2746
www.tourism.gov.on.ca

Six Nations Tourism
1-866-393-3001
www.sixnationstourism.com

**Southern Ontario
Tourism Organization**
1-800-267-3399
www.SouthernOntario.org

St. Jacobs Country
1-800-265-3353
www.stjacobs.com

TRAIL MANAGEMENT

Grand River Conservation Authority
(519) 621-2761

City of Brantford
(519) 756-1500

City of Cambridge
(519) 740-4681

City of Guelph
(519) 837-5618

City of Kitchener
(519) 741-2382

City of Waterloo
(519) 886-2310

Township of Woolwich
(519) 669-1647

Ontario Ministry of Natural Resources
(519) 826-4955

SUPPORTING TRAILS THROUGH DONATIONS

Grand River Conservation Founation
1-877-29-GRAND

Brant Waterways Foundation
(519) 753-0053

Walter Bean Grand River Trail
(519) 883-4104

Trans Canada Trail
1-800-465-3636

TRAIL FEATURES

TCT = Trans-Canada Trail WB = Walter Bean Trail
RR = Royal Recreation Trail G = Grand Valley Trail
GR = Grand River Tributaries

Grand River Country Trail	Canoeing	Snowshoeing	Cycling	Cross Country Skiing	Horseback Riding	Viewing Area	Group Trail Bookings	Handicapped Access	Camping	Heritage Site	Special Events	Interpretative/ Nature Centre	Links to Major Trails	Birding	Wetland	Carolinian Forest	Grand River	Fossils/ Geology	Page #
Anndale Trail, Waterloo	✓	✓	✓			✓								✓	✓				14
Benham Tract, Fergus		✓												✓					16
Bootlegger Trail, Grand Valley		✓	✓	✓		✓								✓	✓		✓		18
Breithaupt Trail, Kitchener		✓												✓					20
Chesney Hemlock Trail, Drumbo						✓								✓	✓				22
Chicopee Trail, Kitchener	✓			✓	✓	✓								✓	✓				24
Chickadee Trail, Guelph Lake		✓		✓		✓	✓		✓		✓	✓	RR	✓	✓		GR		26
Clair Hills - Westside Trail, Waterloo		✓	✓	✓				✓					WB	✓	✓				28
CNR Spurline Trail, Guelph		✓	✓	✓										✓					30
Devil's Creek Trail, Cambridge		✓	✓	✓										✓	✓		GR	✓	32
Driftwood Trail, Kitchener		✓	✓	✓				✓						✓	✓				34
Elora Cataract Trailway, Belwood Lake to Orton		✓	✓										TCT	✓	✓		✓		36
Foulds Trail, Cambridge			✓											✓	✓				38

TRAIL FEATURES

TCT = Trans-Canada Trail   WB = Walter Bean Trail   G = Grand Valley Trail
RR = Royal Recreation Trail   G = Grand Valley Trail
GR = Grand River Tributaries

Trail	Page #	Fossils/Geology	Grand River	Carolinian Forest	Wetland	Birding	Links to Major Trails	Interpretative/Nature Centre	Special Events	Heritage Site	Camping	Handicapped Access	Group Trail Bookings	Viewing Area	Horseback Riding	Cross Country Skiing	Cycling	Snowshoeing	Canoeing
Gordon Glaves - Waterworks Park Trail, Brantford	40		✓	✓			TCT					✓		✓			✓		
Jacob's Landing Trail, Cambridge	42		GR		✓	✓				✓							✓	✓	
Kissing Bridge Trailway, Elmira	44		GR		✓	✓	TCT								✓	✓	✓	✓	
Lakeside Park Trail, Kitchener	46		✓		✓	✓				✓						✓	✓	✓	
Linear Trail, Cambridge	48					✓				✓							✓		
Little Tract Trail, Cambridge	50				✓	✓											✓		
Maryhill Cycling Trail, Bloomingdale	52		GR			✓	TCT										✓		
Mill Race Trail, St. Jacobs	54		GR			✓				✓							✓		
Mill Run Trail, Cambridge	56	✓	GR		✓	✓											✓		
RIM Park Trail, Waterloo	58		✓		✓	✓	WB			✓		✓				✓	✓	✓	
Riverside Park Loop, Cambridge	60		GR		✓	✓			✓	✓	✓								
Rockway Gardens Trail, Kitchener	62					✓	RR		✓										
Rockwood - Gilbert MacIntyre Trail, Rockwood	64	✓	GR		✓	✓				✓				✓			✓		
Royal Recreation Downtown Trail, Guelph	66		GR			✓				✓									✓

TRAIL FEATURES

TCT = Trans-Canada Trail   WB = Walter Bean Trail
RR = Royal Recreation Trail   G = Grand Valley Trail
GR = Grand River Tributaries

Trail	Page #	Fossils/Geology	Grand River	Carolinian Forest	Wetland	Birding	Links to Major Trails	Interpretive/Nature Centre	Special Events	Heritage Site	Camping	Handicapped Access	Group Trail Bookings	Viewing Area	Horseback Riding	Cross Country Skiing	Cycling	Snowshoeing	Canoeing
Ruthven Riverside Trail, Cayuga	68		✓	✓		✓	G	✓	✓	✓				✓		✓	✓	✓	✓
S.C. Johnson Trail, Paris to Brantford	70		✓	✓		✓	TCT			✓		✓				✓	✓	✓	✓
Schneider's Greenway Trail, Kitchener	72		GR			✓											✓	✓	
Shade's Mills Trail, Cambridge	74		GR		✓	✓		✓					✓			✓		✓	
Silver Lake Trail, Waterloo	76			✓	✓	✓	TCT			✓								✓	
Speed River Trail, Guelph	78		GR			✓	RR												
Taquanyah Nature Centre Trail, Cayuga	80		GR		✓	✓		✓	✓										
Victoria Woods Trail, Guelph	82				✓	✓		✓	✓				✓			✓	✓	✓	
Walter Bean: Economical Insurace Trailway, Waterloo	84		✓			✓										✓	✓	✓	
Walter Bean: J.A. Pollock Family Trailway, Kitchener	86		✓			✓	TCT									✓	✓	✓	
Walter Bean Trailhead, Cambridge	88	✓	✓	✓		✓													
Woolwich Reservoir Elmira Lions Trail, Elmira	90		GR			✓				✓							✓		
West Montrose Cycling Trail	92		✓			✓													

101

INDEX

Alphabetical Trail Listing